Studying CHILDHOOD

Jennie Petersen

MACMILLAN

First published 1991

Published by
MACMILLAN EDUCATION LTD
Houndmills, Basingstoke, Hampshire RG21 2XS
and London
Companies and representatives
throughout the world

Designed by
Raynor Design
Long Compton

Printed in Hong Kong

British Library Cataloguing in Publication Data
Petersen, Jennie
Studying childhood.
1. Children. Psychology
I. Title
155.4
ISBN 0–333–52157–9

Acknowledgements

The author and publishers wish to thank the following who have kindly given permission for the use of copyright material:

Advertising Standards Authority Ltd. for extracts from the British Code of Advertising Practice; Churchill Livingstone, Inc. for the figure showing Infant Mortality Rates per Thousand Live Births; The Controller of Her Majesty's Stationery Office for material from *Social Trends 17 and 19*, 1987 and 1989; and the chart, 'Elderly People in Residential Accommodation'; Express Newspapers plc. for 'And baby makes three in our happiest family', *Daily Express*, 13.4.89 and 'Farewell, au pair pal', *Daily Express*, 18.4.89; Hamish Hamilton Ltd. for 'Running Water' by Minou Drouet from *First Poems*, 1956; Health Education Authority for adapted material from *My Body* Project; Ewan MacNaughton Associates for 'Putting Safety First', *The Daily Telegraph*, 18.7.88; Simon and Schuster International Group for material from *Science 5–13*, Macdonald Children's; Solo Syndication for material from 'Meet the most caring kids in Britain', *Woman*, 8.5.89, 'Dear Gill', *Woman's Realm*, 4.2.89, 'Funny of the week', *Woman's Realm*, 14.2.89, 'Inside a pre-school profit centre', *Daily Mail*, 4.2.89, and 'Joanne, the little lifesaver, gets her reward', *Daily Mail*, 11.4.89; Thames Television Help Programme for material from *Violence Breeds Violence: The Case Against* Smoking by Penelope Leach and Peter Newell, EPOCH; Times Newspapers Ltd. for material from 'Drive to help mothers at work in 1990's' by Robin Oakley and Roland Rudd, *The Times*, 27.11.88, copyright © Times Newspapers Ltd. 1988; and 'Boy of 9 sexually assaulted pensioner' by Craig Seton, *The Times*, 13.4.89, 'Easy Credit 'destroying families through debt'' by Ruth Gledhill, *The Times*, 9.5.89, 'Sex abuse cases up by 24%' by Ruth Gledhill, *The Times*, 13.4.89, 'Doctor's concern as five Cleveland cases are reopened' by Peter Davenport, *The Times*, 8.5.89, copyright © Times Newspapers Ltd. 1989; Unwin Hyman Ltd. for table, 'Stages of Reading Development' from *Understanding Child Development* by Sara Meadows; John Wiley & Sons, Inc. for figure from *Children: Development Through Adolescence* by Alison Clarke, p. 296.

The author and publishers wish to acknowledge, with thanks, the following photographic sources:

Associated Press: p. 58; John Birdsall Photography: pp. 4, 83; British Airways: p. 82; Rex Features; Mary Evans Picture Library: p. 34; Richard and Sally Greenhill: pp. 81, 90; John and Penny Hubley: p. 61; NCH: pp. 5, 8, 9, 12, 16, 33, 34; 44, 62, 74, 80, 81, 86, 116; Mansell Collection: p. 116; Mail Newspapers plc: p. 17; The Press Association; Scotsman Publications: p. 24; Topham Picture Library: p. 61.

Every effort has been made to trace all the copyright holders but if any have been inadvertently overlooked the publishers will be pleased to make the necessary arrangement at the first opportunity.

Contents

Acknowledgements   2
Letter to students   4
Record chart   6

Part 1   Investigations

1 **Investigational assignments**
   1 What is a child?   8
   2 Is that a fact?   10
   3 What influences how a child
      develops?   11
   4 How important is a young child's
      environment?   14
   5 What do children need to learn?   16
   6 How can adults help children to
      learn?   19
   7 Should children be punished if they are
      naughty?   21
   8 What is child abuse?   23
   9 Is it difficult to bring up children?   27
   10 Whose job is it to look after the welfare
      of children?   30
   11 Who should look after these
      children?   30
   12 Should children work?   34
   13 What are the hazards?   38
   14 Should children be the targets of
      commercial advertising?   39
   15 How can young children's health be
      ensured?   42

2 **Investigational homeworks**   43

3 **How do you get an investigational idea
   of your own?**   48

Part 2   Technological assignments

4 **Questioning the effects of technology**
   1 What is technology?   54

2 Does technology affect childhood?   58
3 Does technology affect the everyday
   life of children?   59
4 Does technology affect children's
   learning at school?   61

5 **The technological process**
   1 Analysing problems to be solved   63
   2 Getting vague ideas recorded   64
   3 Choosing the best idea   66
   4 Making a prototype   67
   5 Testing your prototype   69
   6 Evaluating the technological
      process   69

6 **Technological assignments 1–12**   74

Part 3   Methodology

7 **Methodological assignments**
   1 Making comparisons   90
   2 Correlations   92
   3 Observing children   94
   4 Writing a case study   96
   5 Conducting a survey   98
   6 Interviewing people   99
   7 Taking measurements   100
   8 Writing an investigational report   102

8 **Some investigations by professional
   researchers**   110

9 **Investigations by students**   115

10 **Exercises in converting data into
   graphical form**   120

Further reading   126

Letter to teacher/lecturer   128

Dear Students

I am getting older now and my children are grown-up. The future is yours rather than mine. You will be the adults who produce and protect the next generation. This book has been written for you to study some of the important issues about children. Whether you become a parent or not, the assignments will help you to think about the responsibilities that all adults have towards children.

There is no one right way to bring up children. Many entirely different methods of caring for, protecting and educating children are equally successful. This book is not going to tell you how to bring up a child if you do become a parent. What I hope it will do is to help you to make decisions in the future about the welfare of children, whether they be your own or others.

There are many agencies and organisations that are concerned with the welfare of children. You probably know about some of the better-known ones. One of these

organisations, the National Children's Home (NCH), has contributed in the production of this book. They have helped in a number of ways – providing materials, photographs and ideas – because they too feel strongly that you are the future and only you can make it better for the next generation. It is a great responsibility that you need education for.

Your own experience of childhood is valuable when studying children. You will be able to use your experiences to help others learn. You will probably find that some parts of this book will make you think quite a lot about yourself and your future.

It has been divided into three sections. They are entitled 'Investigations', 'Technological Assignments' and 'Methodology'. You may not necessarily start at the beginning and work your way through each section because your teachers might plan to use different sections to fit different courses or modules that you are studying. The 'Investigations' section contains assignments that would be suitable for many courses offered in school that help you to think about the human condition and develop your personal and social skills. Technology is a major part of all pupils' learning and the section called 'Technological Assignments' should help you to appreciate what technology is and its implications for childhood, as well as give you practice of it when designing things

(artefacts), systems and environments that affect children and their families. The final section is about the methodology used in research about childhood. The assignments in this section are there to help you become more aware of how you might tackle a research-based investigation and give you the experience of some of the skills you need to be able to do that. If you have a GCSE investigation to do as part of the course you are studying this section should help you to do it well.

If you need to, there is no reason why you cannot use this book as an individual. However, it has been written with the hope that you will work with others on the majority of tasks. Symbols at the top of each investigation suggest whether it is best suited for the whole class, for groups or for individuals.

whole class   group   individual

Every whole class and group investigation will start with a brief statement of what you should learn by being involved in it. You may like to keep a record of your learning and achievements as you work through the different activities. This should help you to decide how much and how well you are learning. There are many ways that you could do this. Some people prefer to compile a diary about their learning, writing brief notes after each session on what they did well, what they found difficult and how successful their efforts were. Others prefer to keep track of the skills they are practising, the topics they have covered and the types of choices they have made. One way of doing this is to tick boxes on a prepared record sheet. For those students who wish to do this, an example is given at the end of this letter. You may prefer to devise your own record chart.

I very much hope that you will find the work in this book a serious and interesting part of your studies.

Yours sincerely,

Jennie Petersen

Jennie Petersen

Record chart

Name

Personal

I could use my own experience in this work.											
I understood the tasks.											
I learned something new.											
I taught somebody else something they did not know before.											
The work made me think about my future.											
I did some extra work for this.											

Group

I contributed well to my group's work.											
I was able to explain my ideas to the others.											
I was glad to have others to work with.											
My group helped me to understand something.											
I was able to help others understand something.											
We were able to criticise our own work.											
I found out that other people have very different ideas from myself.											

The Tasks

Were fun.											
Were interesting.											
Were rather difficult.											
Were too simple.											

PART
1

Investigations

Investigational assignments

1 What is a child?

What you should learn	**What you will need**
• Words can mean different things to different people • That your own experience of childhood is a valuable part of studying children • That sharing some memories and feelings can help you to understand yourself better	A double lesson (about 1 hour 10 minutes) A ruler Display card Pencil Glue Paper Scissors

Look carefully at this diagram. It is a simplified way of studying what has happened to a girl called Ruth during the first twenty years of her life.

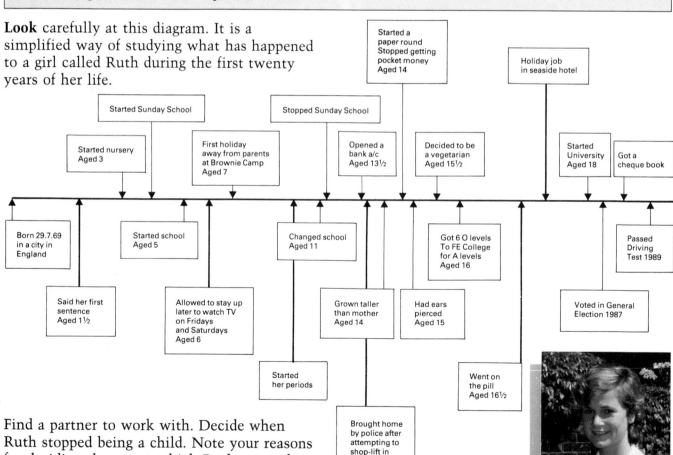

Find a partner to work with. Decide when Ruth stopped being a child. Note your reasons for deciding the age at which Ruth stopped being a child.

Now look at another lifeline. This one is of a boy called Carlos.

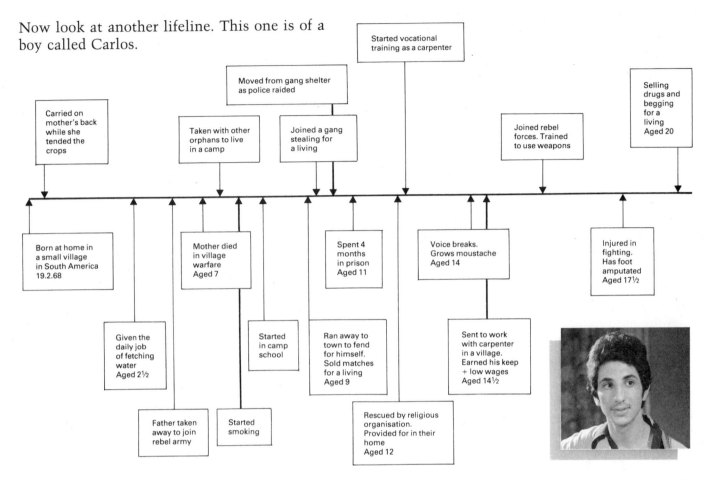

Carried on mother's back while she tended the crops

Moved from gang shelter as police raided

Started vocational training as a carpenter

Taken with other orphans to live in a camp

Joined a gang stealing for a living

Joined rebel forces. Trained to use weapons

Selling drugs and begging for a living Aged 20

Born at home in a small village in South America 19.2.68

Mother died in village warfare Aged 7

Spent 4 months in prison Aged 11

Voice breaks. Grows moustache Aged 14

Injured in fighting. Has foot amputated Aged 17½

Given the daily job of fetching water Aged 2½

Started in camp school

Ran away to town to fend for himself. Sold matches for a living Aged 9

Sent to work with carpenter in a village. Earned his keep + low wages Aged 14½

Father taken away to join rebel army

Started smoking

Rescued by religious organisation. Provided for in their home Aged 12

Decide when Carlos stopped being a child. Decide whether your reasons were the same for both Ruth and Carlos.

By yourself, **decide** whether you think you are a child or not. It may help you to draw your own lifeline first. You could make two lists: one list of the reasons why you feel you are still a child, and the other list the reasons why you feel you are not a child any more.

Share your decision and the reasons with someone else. Find out whether you have made similar decisions with similar reasons. **Read** the following definitions of a child:

'A child is every human being up to the age of 18 unless, under the law of his/her state, he/she has attained the age of majority earlier.'
United Nations: Rights of the Child, 1989

'A child is a human from birth to puberty.'
Dictionary, 1970

Are these definitions good enough? Is it only a matter of age or physical maturity?

Read the following quotations about children:

'When I was a child, I spake as a child, I understood as a child, I thought as a child: but when I became a man, I put away childish things.'
Bible

'I hold it indisputable, that the first duty of a State is to see that every child born therein shall be well housed, clothed, fed, and educated, till it attain years of discretion.'
John Ruskin, 1819–1900

Both of those quotations seem to be saying that there is something more than age and physical maturity about the difference between a child and an adult.

Write your own definition of a child. When you have finished stick your idea on the class display along with all the others.

Choose which of the following tasks you would like to do. You can do this either by yourself or with a partner.

1 Write a letter to your MP giving reasons why you think that the age of majority in the UK should be changed from 18 years.

2   Write a poem or the lyrics for a song explaining why you like being a child.

3   Draw a picture that shows what it feels like to be the age you are.

4   Explain to a partner how you think an adolescent who has broken the law should be dealt with by society. Should they be held responsible or treated like a child? Write a list of your reasons.

Communicate with the whole class about what you have been thinking. You can do this by making a display of your work for others to read and look at. If time allows you could discuss your work. It might be interesting to construct a Venn diagram showing how many of your class feel themselves to be entirely adult, how many feel themselves to be entirely a child and how many feel they are a mixture of child and adult. The Venn diagram could also be displayed with your work.

2 Is that a fact?

What you should learn

- To be able to distinguish between fact and opinion
- To listen carefully to the opinions of others
- To identify sources of reliable information

What you will need

A double lesson   Some large sheets of paper
Paper   Some newspapers/
Pen/pencil/   magazines
highlighter pens   Glue

Read the following definitions:

A **fact** is something that is proven to be true; eg, all teenagers are between 13 and 19 years old.

An **opinion** is someone's view; eg, all teenagers are lazy.

A **myth** is a common belief that something is true, when there is no evidence that it is; eg, teenage boys don't wash unless they are forced to.

With a partner, see if you can **write** down a fact, an opinion and a myth about childhood.

Join in with another pair. Share your examples with each other. If, as a result of discussing them you would like to change them, do so.

Go through the following statements and decide whether or not each one is a fact, an opinion or a myth.

1   Very young children cannot control their bladders.
2   Babies often sleep during part of the day.
3   Children need to run around and let off steam.
4   Children need toys to play with in order to develop well.
5   Babies are born blind.
6   Children need more sleep than adults.
7   Children should be brought up to be polite and friendly to everyone.
8   Added salt on food in their diet is dangerous for children.
9   All children should be able to read by the time they are 7 years old.
10 Human embryos can be frozen and still survive to develop into children.
11 Hard work never hurt anyone.
12 Babies should not sleep on their stomachs.
13 Young children learn about their world through their senses.
14 Fat babies are healthy babies.
15 Babies get cold very quickly if they are exposed to a cold environment.
16 Children should be seen and not heard.
17 Spare the rod and spoil the child.
18 Rewarding children for good behaviour works better than punishing them for bad behaviour.
19 Children can get married in the UK.
20 Babies born with a caul over their heads will never die of drowning.

Decide as a group whether that was difficult to do. Write down why it was difficult. Were some of the statements easier than others to categorise? Write down which ones your group were able to agree about easily.

Many people believe everything they read. They forget that much of what is published in newspapers and magazines is opinion. Opinions are interesting. We often want to know what other people think about certain things – it's one of the ways we get to know people. True facts are sometimes more difficult to get reliable information about.

Still working in your group of four, **make a list** of places, things and people that can be used to try and find out the truth. Once you have finished the list, go over it and underline those that you think are the most reliable sources of factual information. Share your group's ideas with the rest of the class.

As an individual, write a fact, an opinion and a myth about families. **Ask** a friend if they agree

that you have written one of each. If you both agree, then stick yours on to a class poster ready to display. Try and find time to read what other people have written.

If you have time you could:
1 Look through some newspaper and magazine articles and highlight the opinions in blue, the facts in pink/red and any myths in yellow.
2 Write or record on audiocassette a short and entirely factual description of yourself or a young child you know well.
3 Write or record a short and entirely opinion-based description of your school or college or a club you belong to.
4 Decide what evidence could be collected to disprove the myth that teenage boys don't wash unless they are forced to. Make a list of the ways you could do it.

All these could be put into your classroom display.

3 What influences how a child develops? ◇◇

What you should learn

- That we are all a mixture of our biology and our upbringing
- That things are not always as they seem

What you will need

Two double lessons Paper	Pen/pencils/markers – various colours Large sheets of paper

Work in groups of five to six people. On a large sheet of paper, **draw** a small child in the middle of the sheet. One of your group should then write down around the child all the ideas you can of the things, experiences and people who will influence how a child develops. Take enough time to generate at least twenty different ideas. If your group is really thinking well you may well come up with many more.

Discuss which, of all your group's ideas, you think are the most important influences on a child. When you have all agreed, underline those in a colour. Decide whether or not a child is born with anything that will influence her or his development. Make a list of what you think nature gives to a child.

Most children learn to walk and talk quite naturally. They learn the language of the people they are brought up by. It seems that all children are born with the ability to learn to speak and understand when they are spoken to, yet if they are not given opportunities to listen and try out language, that inborn potential seems to fade away.

Read the following descriptions of children who have had a most unusual upbringing.

Abandoned children brought up by animals

There are several well-known studies of children who had been abandoned for various reasons and were adopted by animals. The most famous studies are concerned with wolves. These children were rescued as young adults. They had been socialised as wolves. They ate raw meat as wolves did, tearing the flesh with their teeth. They were as good at moving about on all fours as on two feet and communicated in grunts and snarls as would any wolf. They were completely uncivilised, defecating and urinating as animals. Their skin was tough and dirty. On being rescued by kindly and caring people they were never completely socialised. They never learned to speak and caught human diseases very easily. They all died at an early age from these diseases.

Genie

Genie's father was a bully. He physically abused his wife and children and kept them isolated from the community they lived in. Although normal except for a hip defect, Genie, he decided, was retarded. He put her away in a bare room in the family home. She was kept there for eleven years with the door bolted and the curtains drawn. Most of the time Genie was kept naked and strapped to a potty chair. She was fed baby food by one member of the family who entered the room for only long enough to do this. She had no toys, only a few magazines to look at. If she made any noise she was beaten. In 1970, after a violent argument with her husband, her mother managed to telephone Genie's grandmother who came and rescued them both. Genie was 13 years old at the time. At this age she was unable to stand erect, walk, talk, chew solid food or control her bodily functions. With sympathetic care and training Genie rapidly progressed. She learned to eat more normally, to use the lavatory and to walk. More slowly, she began to understand what was said to her and to talk. However, her language development never progressed further than the level of a 4–5-year-old child.

Discuss those descriptions and think about how those children adapted to the environment they found themselves in.

For a long while scientists have been intrigued by how much of a person is the result of their biological, genetic make-up and how much is to do with the environment they grew up in. It is a very difficult thing to find out. The researchers tried to answer the question by studying identical twins who had been separated at birth.

Identical twins are born with exactly the same genetic make-up as each other. This is because one egg from the mother has been fertilised by one sperm from the father *before* it divides equally into two embryos. Thus two identical babies are made. Researchers studying identical twins who had been brought up in different environments thought that any major differences between them would be entirely due to their upbringing.

Professor Bouchard from the University of Minnesota in Minneapolis brought many divided sets of twins together for the first time. In most cases they did not even know they had a twin until the research programme informed them. When he brought them together he discovered the following:

Oscar and Jack

Separated at six months. One was brought up as a Jew in Trinidad. The other was a member of the Hitler Youth in Germany. They met after 46 years.

- At their first meeting both wore identical rectangular wire-rimmed spectacles with rounded corners.
- Both wore blue shirts with breast pockets and epaulettes.
- Both read magazines back to front.
- Both absent-mindedly store rubber bands on their wrists.
- Both like reading in restaurants.
- Both have fits of anger.
- Both had the odd joke of sneezing loudly to watch the reactions of others.

The Giggle Twins

Separated at birth. One brought up in Hammersmith, the other in Luton. They met after 41 years.

- Both tinted their greying hair with the same shade of auburn.
- Both enjoyed the novels of Alistair MacLean and Catherine Cookson.
- Both used to read *My Weekly* and then stopped.
- Both clutch the bannister for fear of falling downstairs.
- Both met their future husbands at town hall dances when they were sixteen.
- Both married in their early twenties.
- Both had big autumn weddings.
- Both worked in local government as did their husbands.
- Both laugh more than anyone else they know.
- Both had a miscarriage with their first pregnancy.
- Both are careful about money.

- Both have the favourite colour of blue.
- Both hated games and maths at school.
- Both had been Girl Guides.
- Both had fallen downstairs aged 15 years old and had developed weak ankles.
- Both had taken ballroom dancing lessons.
- Both have a history of fad diets and put on weight very easily.
- Both drink their coffee black and cold with no sugar.
- Both love chocolates and liqueurs.
- Both hate heights and are squeamish about blood.
- Both have no sense of direction.
- Both arrived at their first meeting wearing a beige dress and a brown velvet jacket.
- Both have a habit of pushing up their noses, which they both call 'squidging'.

Decide which of these things could have been a coincidence and which more likely to be due to their genetic inheritance.

Some further work you could do:
1   Write or record a description of how you feel your upbringing has affected your development.
2   Write two lists, one of the things about you that you think you have inherited from your parents, and the other about those things about your upbringing that made you different to your parents.
3   Read more about Wolf Children. See page 127 for further reading.
4   Interview a pair of twins to find out how similar or different they are. You can find twins of any age to interview.

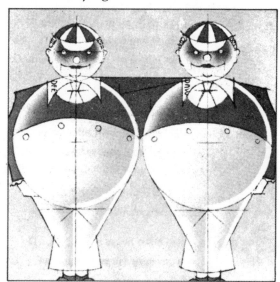

4 How important is a young child's environment? ◇◇

What you should learn

- To analyse a descriptive text
- To be self-critical
- To share ideas in a formal way
- To contribute to a group effort

What you will need

Two double lessons   Acting props
Pencil   OHP transparencies
Paper   Large sheets of paper
Access to materials for presentation:
OHP pens; marker pens in various colours

Read the following case study about a young man called Dave.

In your group, **make a list** of all the factors in the case study that were, in your opinion, good about his childhood environment. Give your reasons why you think as you do.

Make another list of the factors which you feel did not help Dave during his childhood. Give your reasons.

DAVE

Born in 1974 to an Irish mother married to a Scottish father twenty years older than his wife. When they married, these parents rented a small flat in the outer suburbs of north-west London. Dave was born in hospital after a long labour and was delivered with the help of forceps. He weighed 2.8kg and was breast fed for a few weeks before his mother changed to bottle feeding because she wanted to get back to her work as a secretary. Dave's father was, at the time, unemployed. At the age of two, when Dave's father found work as a salesman, a childminder was found to look after Dave during the day. At the weekends the family would make frequent trips to the countryside around London where his parents hoped, one day, to buy a home. At the age of four Dave was a big, healthy child attending the nursery class of the local infants school. In 1978 Dave's father died leaving his wife and child living in the small rented flat. Dave was taken by his mother to live in Northern Ireland with his grandparents. After four years at primary school it was clear that Dave was not doing very well. He could barely read, had few friends and had become a fearful child, teased by the other children at school. Dave's mother found work in Northern Ireland and eventually met a kind man, near her own age, who she married in 1986. They moved into a tiny cottage just a few yards from Dave's grandparents' home leaving Dave to live with the grandparents whose house was much larger than the little cottage. By this time Dave was attending the local secondary school and receiving special help with his learning difficulties. He saw his mother every day after school before he went home for his tea. Dave left school at 16 with a school record of achievement that included a good report of his hard work, honesty and general behaviour; virtually no academic qualifications; an adult first-aid certificate; a pre-driver's certificate and a gold award for life-saving. He had a few loyal friends who lived locally. He started a Youth Training Scheme at 17 years and hoped eventually to work as a carpenter like his stepfather.

Now, read about Sammy.

SAMMY

○ Sammy was born early in 1973. Her father was a GP in a small market town in the West Midlands. Her mother had been a nurse at Great Ormond Street Hospital before her marriage, but since then she had stayed at home helping her husband with his work and bringing up a family of three. Sammy was their middle child, having an older sibling called Mike and a younger one called Shaun. Mike was born in 1972 and Shaun in 1976. Sammy was born at home after a short labour. She was breast-fed until weaning was complete and apart from being very small for her age was a healthy and lively toddler. Her parents were heavily mortgaged as they had bought a large house on the outskirts of the town. Much of Sammy's pre-school life was spent playing in their large garden with her brothers and neighbours' children. When Mike was 7½ years old, he was sent away to boarding school. Sammy attended her small school in the town once she was 5 years old. When she was in the junior section of her school she appeared to be progressing well. It was at this time that her younger brother was sent off to join Mike at his boarding school. Sammy missed the company at home but was encouraged to take her many friends home to play. She usually just had to ask her mother and arrangements were made. Sammy learned easily and quickly, but much preferred messing about with her friends. She had to be persuaded to attend to her school work, particularly to the homework she'd been set. She saw very little of her father who was perpetually busy either with his patients or the various committees he was involved with. When Sammy was 10 she was given a computer which she kept in her bedroom along with many games, books and toys. In 1986 Sammy was sent to a girls' boarding school by the seaside. She quickly made new friends at the new school. When she was 14, however, she was expelled from the

○ school, having been found using an illegal substance on the school premises. Her parents were extremely angry about this episode and having arranged for her to attend the local secondary school, they kept a very strict eye on who she was friendly with and where she was. In 1989 Sammy left home. She took with her a suitcase full of clothes, make-up, music tapes, some money she had stolen from her father's study and her GCSE certificate of an A, 3 Ds and an F. She is at present working in MacDonalds in Birmingham and shares a bedsitter with her boyfriend. Mike is an art student living in London and Shaun is awaiting the results of his GCSEs.

Look at what you wrote on your list after you read about Dave. Decide whether the same factors seem important in Sammy's case. If they don't, list the positive and negative factors in Sammy's development.

Prepare a short presentation of your group's answer to the question 'How important is a young child's environment?'. Use the two case studies to decide:

1 whether all children need certain environmental conditions for their well-being.
2 what Dave and Sammy's parents could have done to make things better for their children.
3 what could be changed in society to make a better environment for developing children.

When preparing your presentation you should consider what would be the best method to use to communicate your ideas; who, within the group, is going to present what and how can you use the different skills your group members have.

Some ideas for how you might like to present your ideas

- As a talk
- As visual information such as OHP, cartoons, drawings
- In dramatic form, eg. role playing Dave or Sammy's mother
- As an interview with a politician or some parents or a headteacher.

When all the presentations have been done, spend some time deciding which methods worked the best. As an individual, **think** about your contribution to your group's work. If you feel you didn't contribute as much as you could, note the reasons why. Is there anything that you could do to make it better next time? You might like to discuss this with your teacher or the other members of the group. You might conclude that you did too much of the work involved. Think about how this came about. Could you make it different another time? If time allows you could choose one of the following to do:

1   Choose some music that might have matched
  (a) Dave's mood when he learned that his mother was going to move out leaving him with his grandparents.
  (b) Sammy's feelings when she made her decision to leave home.
2   Write a list of the advantages of being able to let children have their own bedrooms.
3   Write a short report for the Personnel Department stating why you, as the interviewing officer, have appointed Dave to a post as a junior carpenter. You need to justify your decision.
4   Role-play, with a partner, a conversation between Sammy's mother and father about Sammy's lifestyle in Birmingham.

5 What do children need to learn? ◈

What you *should* learn

- That learning is a complex process concerning knowledge, skills and attitudes
- That some things are easier to learn than others
- That individuals vary when deciding which things they find difficult to learn

What you *will* need

A double lesson	Large sheets of paper
Paper	Markers
Pen/pencil/colours	

As children develop they gradually learn and make sense of the world as they find it. **Look** at some of the results of this learning shown on the next two pages:

One day I was caught in a shower with my small granddaughter. Quickly I pulled up her anorak hood. She looked so sad as she remarked, "Poor Granny, you haven't got a lid."
Roma Broomfield, Bashley, Hants

Poem by Minou Dronet. Aged 8 years in 1955.

Running Water

I love the water that does not last
whose sentence is never ended
whose shape whose voice
is never the same
one day I'll curl up in her skirts
and I'll be lost
like a chicken
in the egg
and I'll be the tiny autumn leaf
colour of sunshine
and blood
and what is already no more
and I'll make myself light and willing
so that the sea and the wind
that I love
will carry me always away
somewhere else.

p. 18. First Poems (Hamish Hamilton Ltd, 1956)

SUZANNE DRISCOLL wiped away a tear of pride yesterday as she watched daughter Joanne, aged five, honoured for saving her life.

Joanne and her sister, three-year-old Lee-Anne, acted swiftly the day Mrs Driscoll collapsed with a stroke in the bathroom.

The girls at first tried to revive her by feeding her water and toothpaste. When that failed, they tried to fetch help but the outside doors were locked. There was no phone in the house but Joanne wasn't beaten.

She opened the bathroom window, dropped several feet to the ground and ran for assistance.

Yesterday Joanne, of Crossgate, Leeds, collected a good citizens award from the Lord Mayor of London, Sir Christopher Collet.

He said: 'You did a remarkably brave thing.' She said: 'I helped Mummy the only way I could.'

Joanne, the little lifesaver, gets her reward

WILD CHILD: Rough and tumble way of life for young travellers

THE RAGGLE TAGGLE KIDS

"Our children are like wild animals" - mother

"HAVE you come to bring us toilets?" cry the traveller children as they run round and round us in rings.

"The person who has come to bring them toilets" seems to be the only one from outside their fenced-in little inner city world they are prepared to respect.

But they are fascinated when someone dares step into their territory. They shout abuse, then, growing brave, come closer. If you do not draw away they try and touch you feeling your fingers for rings, your pocket for coins and your bag for holes.

It is not possible to be romantic about these children.

Even a traveller woman, shaking her head, says: "The children are like wild animals.

Playing shops, and it's all in a good cause

CHILDREN at the Garden Suburb Infants School held a bring and buy toy sale and raised £109 towards the Blue Peter appeal in aid of Kampuchea, formerly Cambodia. Here Diana Onchere, 7, digs deep in her purse to buy from salesgirl Joanna Levine, 6.

As a group, **list** all the things you think children should learn in order to manage as an adult in society. You should be able to write down a large number of knowledge areas, skills and attitudes.

When you have finished, discuss which are the most important in your opinion. Mark the twenty most important with an asterisk.

Using your list of the twenty most important things, try to **categorise** them into those mainly physical, mainly intellectual, emotional and moral. Some of your items may belong in more than one category. For example, you may have chosen 'Being able to write' as an important skill. The skill of writing is a physical, intellectual and social skill. In order to write you need control over the muscles of your hand to achieve it. You also need your brain working well so that you remember how to form your letters, distinguish them from others and create meaningful sentences. Without social experience it would be difficult to give your writing any meaning.

Now **decide** which items on your list are the easiest to learn – use a colour to distinguish these; which ones are the hardest to learn – use a different colour for these.

On a large sheet of paper, write a chart that shows your twenty most important things to be learned; how difficult they are to learn well and your reasons for saying so.

Finally, decide which has the biggest influence on whether or not a child would learn these things. Is it the family, the education system or the community? Write your main ideas about this on a large sheet of paper.

Display the results of the group's thoughts and discussions.

Read carefully the other groups' work prior to reviewing your own group's work. You may find that you have changed your mind about some points.

Before you finish this assignment, as a whole class decide which group's list best describes the most important things a child needs to learn. In the next assignment you will use that list to work with. A quick way of deciding is for you to go and stand by the list you prefer.

The one chosen is the one with the most people standing by it. However, you may wish to spend more time discussing the choice. You may feel that you want to use a mixture from different groups to find the best list.

If you have time, you could:
1   Make a list of the knowledge, skills and attitudes already demonstrated by the children in the stimulus material presented at the beginning of the assignment.
2   Tell another student about an important learning experience that you had as a young child.
3   Write a critical account of the education system as you have experienced it.
4   Write a letter to your family explaining how much you appreciate being part of it.

6 How can adults help children to learn? ◇◇

What you should learn

- To understand some of your own difficulties with learning
- That everyone finds something difficult to learn
- That there are outside influences working at both helping and hindering learning

What you will need

Your chosen list from last assignment
Paper
Pen/pencil
Someone prepared to take notes of the discussion and talk to another group about what your group thinks.

As a class **decide** which is the best way of dividing the list of twenty important things a child needs to learn, so that each group can work on four or five items. It might be best if the items for each group are linked in some way; eg, all the physical skills or all the things usually learned at home.

Once you have got your group's part of the list, take each item separately and decide:
1   How you learned it (if you have)?
2   Is it an easy thing to learn?

3 What makes it easy or difficult?

4 Who or what has helped you to learn it?

5 How is it helping you now as a young adult?

6 How is it going to help you in the future?

Make a chart or diagram to show how adults can help children to learn each item on your list. You may like to use a diagram like this:

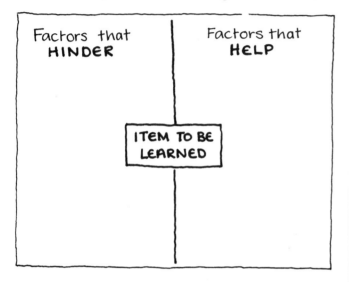

For example, if one item on your list was 'learning to read', you might produce a diagram like this:

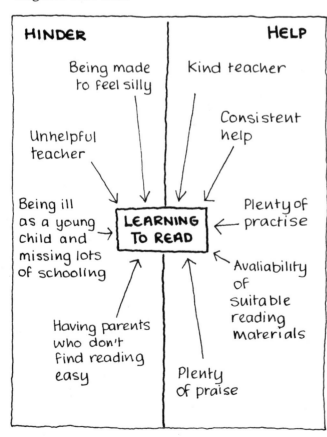

Please note that if 'learning to read' *is* one of the items your group is exploring, the above example has shown only a few of the circumstances that might help or hinder the process of learning to read.

When you have worked on each item on your share of the list, have a look at the diagrams you have made. Spread them out so that you can see them all. Are there any helpful factors that crop up for different items? For example, a kind or strict teacher might be on each one. **Make a list** of common factors.

Are there any improvements to the conditions for learning that society could develop through central or local government and the legal system? For example, in the 'Learning to read' diagram above, would smaller classes in primary schools provide the conditions more conducive to children having a kind teacher, consistent help, plenty of practice and plenty of praise? Would it cost more? Who would find the money? How?

Look at your list again and see if you can **generate** some ideas on how the conditions for learning through the home, the school and community life might be improved and what the implications of those improvements might be.

Share your ideas with another group. One of you should be ready to talk about your group's discussions and have some notes to refer to.

If you want to you could try one of the following:

1 Write a letter to a newpaper arguing the case for increasing community charge levels to allow for smaller classes in primary schools.

2 Compose a poem describing your emotions at finding that something is very difficult to do.

3 Make a list of the events or situations going on in the world that make the future needs of children difficult to predict.

4 Make a greetings card for a child that praises the child for having achieved a simple goal; eg, swimming a width or tidying his or her bedroom unaided. Try to make it so that the child would be really proud of it.

7 Should children be punished if they are naughty? ◈

Look at the situations here and on page 22:

As a group, decide which of these situations can be considered naughty. Compose a definition of naughty behaviour in young children. Then make a list of the situations that you do find to be naughty and give reasons why you think so and suggestions for how you would deal with them.

Discuss what you feel about punishment. You could start off by describing to each other a situation when you were punished.

What do you think should be the punishment for:

1 Shop-lifting goods worth £1
2 Shop-lifting goods worth £25
3 Starting a fight
4 Being late for school or college
5 Being late for work
6 Verbal abuse of another student
7 Verbal abuse of a teacher
8 Verbal abuse of a police officer
9 Writing graffiti on a wall
10 Dropping litter
11 Careless and sloppy homework
12 Not doing the homework at all

Compare with each other your views on what makes you behave badly. Make a list of all the things that help you to behave well.

Decide whether you would rather be punished if you behave badly, or made to feel good if you behave well and your bad behaviour ignored.

Consider the following questions:

Do parents go on loving their children even if they are naughty?

Can parents go on ignoring bad behaviour?

To find out what parents feel about disciplining their children, **design** a questionnaire that you could use with parents to get an overall picture about the discipline of young children.

Whilst designing your questionnaire you should consider what sort of information your questions will elicit. Are you going to get YES and NO answers?

Will everyone understand your questions? Will they have the same meaning for all people? Will your questions get at the truth or are they likely to get responses that people think they ought to say? For example, Do you smack your child? Many people who do smack their children might answer NO because they think that other people will disapprove of it.

Will you need to give people the chance to say how much they believe something? You can use a rating scale on your questionnaire. For example:

Do you praise your children when they do something well?

Often				Very rarely
	✓			
5	4	3	2	1

When you have finished designing your questionnaire, **explain** to another group why you have designed it as it is. What were you hoping to find out by using it? How would you deal with the information you would get in order to say what you have found out?

Ask questions about each other's design. Make suggestions for their improvement.

If you have the opportunity, you might like to try out your questionnaire on a parent, to see whether the questions do elicit the information you require or whether they produce entirely different answers; for example, someone who asked 'Where were you born?' was expecting the name of a geographical location. What they got from some people was 'At home' and 'In hospital'.

Choose one of the following:
1 Write or record on tape a list of rules for how teachers should treat you in order to bring out your best behaviour.
2 Answer the following letter written to a magazine:

> Dear Marge,
> My 4-year-old is getting out of hand. He's rude and difficult to control. What should I do?
> Yours desperately,
> Edie Harcourt.

3 Make a list of the ways that children can be 'rewarded' without being given presents.
4 Design a questionnaire to use with young children to find out what they feel about discipline at home or school.

8 What is child abuse? ◈

What you should learn

- That attitudes towards children change
- That many people are actively involved in helping abused children
- That abuse can take different forms

What you will need

Paper
Pen/pencil
A variety of presentation resources for students to choose from: OHP; large paper; coloured markers; acting props, etc.
Two double lessons

Children can be abused in a variety of ways. The very fact that children are dependent on the adults in their home and community makes them vulnerable. Adults are more powerful than children both physically and in the way they can control their lives. The NSPCC states in its annual report of 1988 that there are four types of abuse:

Emotional abuse: When threats, verbal attacks, shouting and the absence of love and affection hamper the emotional development of the child;

Neglect: When parents fail to meet the basic and essential needs of their children, such as food, clothes, warmth and medical care;

Physical abuse: When someone physically hurts, injures, maims or kills a child;

Sexual abuse: When girls or boys are used by adults to gratify their own sexual needs.

The majority of people are sickened by the cases of child abuse that are reported in the media. However, attitudes towards children have changed throughout history. In historical terms, it is a comparatively recent idea that children should be believed and respected.

Read the following description of a French royal baby in the seventeenth century. This passage comes from a book called *The History of Childhood* by Philippe Aries. Heroard was the family doctor.

'Louis XIII was not yet one year old. He laughed uproariously when his nanny waggled his cock with her fingers. An amusing trick which the child soon copied. Calling a page, he shouted "Hey, there!" and pulled up his robe showing him his cock.

He was one year old: "In high spirits," notes Heroard, "he made everybody kiss his cock. This amused them all." Similarly everyone considered his behaviour towards two visitors, a certain de Bonières and his daughter, highly amusing: "He laughed at him, lifted up his robe and showed him his cock, but even more so to his daughter, for then, holding it and giving his little laugh, he shook the whole of his body up and down." They thought this so funny that the child took care to repeat a gesture which had been a success; in the presence of "a little lady", "he lifted up his coat, and showed her his cock with such fervour that he was quite beside himself. He lay on his back to show her."

Decide whether such behaviour would be acceptable in today's world. Would what the nanny did be considered abusive?

Read the following excerpt from a newspaper article:

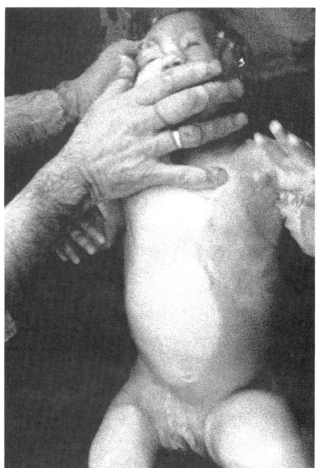

Sheila Kitzinger reports on a man who claims to strengthen infants' physical and mental development by taking them to the limits of pain and endurance

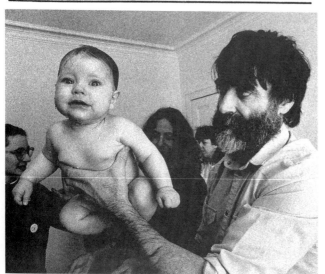

ICE is thick on the rectangular tank. Around it stands an audience of several figures muffled in fur coats, hats, gloves and boots. The tank is in some kind of enclosure — a zoo probably. A man standing on the edge throws a fish into the water. A beluga whale surges up to catch it. Then the man is clutching a naked baby in his grip, suspended by the ankles. He leans forward, separates the chunks of ice, swings the child's body into the air, and plunges the baby head-first into the water.

Swiftly he swings the baby up, it gasps for air, and he flings it under water again.

This is Igor Charkovsky, Russian "water baby expert". He claims that he is strengthening the spine so that the baby will develop faster and better than other babies, both physically and mentally. He says the baby can also commune with whales. He carries out water training on babies from birth, sometimes continuing for years through a child's development.

Read the following excerpt from 'Violence Breeds Violence':

VIOLENCE BREEDS VIOLENCE

THE CASE AGAINST SMACKING

Written by Penelope Leach and Peter Newell of EPOCH

The law protects adults from violence at the hands of anyone else. Why shouldn't it protect children too?

What's so wrong with hitting children?

Most people agree that it is wrong to settle arguments between adult people with blows. And children are people too. Why should they not have equal protection from all forms of violence – particularly when they are among the most vulnerable physically?

Physical punishments are not only wrong, they don't work either. A whack on the bottom may stop a child for that moment. But it won't stop them doing the same thing later on because being hit does not teach anything useful. It doesn't teach children how you want them to behave, and it doesn't teach them to try to please you. Research evidence shows that children who have been slapped or hit are usually so overwhelmed with anger and hurt feelings that they cannot remember what they were punished for.

Most parents in Britain hit their children

A research project at Nottingham University found that 62 per cent of the 700 parents interviewed hit their one-year-old child; almost all (97 per cent) hit their four-year-old – and seven per cent of these four-year-olds are hit at least once a day. By the age of seven, at least eight per cent are being hit once a day and 41 per cent once a week or more. Three-quarters of seven-year-olds are either hit or threatened with an implement (91 per cent of boys and 62 per cent of girls). By the age of 11, 18 per cent are being hit once or more a week. The figures in this research, by John and Elizabeth Newson, which are based on face-to-face interviews are probably underestimates. And they find that hitting is not decreasing. Interviews with a large sample of parents as recently as 1985 found that almost two thirds are still smacking.

What do you mean by 'physical punishment'?

Any action which is meant to cause pain to a child, such as hitting, slapping, smacking, with a hand or with a slipper, strap, stick or other implement is physical punishment. It also includes violent shaking and any kind of forcible imprisonment, such as being locked in a room or cupboard or tied in a cot.

Surely a tap on the legs doesn't count?

Yes it does. Lots of parents 'tap' babies, but many, many more smack four-year-olds. Hitting doesn't work except to relieve parents' feelings. If you let yourself smack your toddler for fiddling with the TV, what can you do when the toddler fiddles again except smack again – harder? And what can you do with the five-year-old who refuses to stay in a bedroom to 'cool off' except lock the door. . .?

Surely you need to use physical force to keep children safe?

There is a difference between using your strength to snatch a child away from a hot stove or prevent them running into a busy road, and intentionally causing pain as punishment.

Won't every parent sometimes lose his or her temper and hit their child?

While hitting children remains acceptable, the answer is probably 'yes' even though hitting other adults (or even pets) is not acceptable. If hitting children was equally unacceptable, most parents would never do it and the few who sometimes did would regret it and try not to.

Is the ordinary kind of smacking that goes on in loving homes worth all this fuss?

Violence does breed violence and is a problem in today's society. Hitting at home is not the only cause of that violence, but there is plenty of evidence to suggest that ending hitting at home would help to reduce it. Children model their behaviour on their parents. Parents who use physical punishment are directly teaching their children that physical force is an acceptable way to get what you want. Research shows a clear link between being hit at home and being a bully at school – and when children who have been physically punished grow up they are more likely to use violence themselves. If we want less violent adults we have to bring them up believing that physical force is not acceptable.

Aren't ordinary physical punishment and child abuse two quite different things?

The acceptance of physical punishment in our society causes a dangerous confusion. When serious cases of child abuse and battering have been investigated, they have often been found to have started with occasional smacks. Also most people responsible for seriously injuring children are found to have been physically punished in their childhood.

Even light blows can accidentally cause serious injury to small children – 'clips round the ear' have burst ear drums and permanently damaged hearing, and smacks catching a child off balance have led to falls and head injuries.

What should replace physical punishment?

Abandoning physical punishment doesn't mean abandoning good behaviour, or consistent limits for children. Rewards work better than punishments for children, just as they do for adults. And the best responses to bad behaviour are those that the child can see are directly linked to it: your immediate disapproval, irritation or anger, the removal of the toy or playmate the child is hurting, or the ending of the game or meal which is being ruined for everyone else.

Read the following Article from the United Nations Convention on the Rights of the Child:

> 'The State Parties to the present Convention shall take all appropriate legislative, administrative, social and educational measures to protect the child from all forms of physical or mental injury or abuse, neglect or negligent treatment, maltreatment or exploitation including sexual abuse, while in the care of the parent(s), legal guardian(s) or any other person who has the care of the child.'

Discuss your feelings about what you have read.

Consider the following issues:
- Why do you think parents allow Igor Tjarkovsky to treat their babies like that?
- Do you agree with the extract from 'Violence Breeds Violence'?
- Who decides what is abusive behaviour towards children? Shouting, for example, could be more acceptable in some cultures than in others. Does sarcasm affect the emotional development of children? How do you feel if someone is sarcastic about your efforts?
- Are some forms of abuse worse than others? Or is it the effect on the child that is the real issue?
- What is best for children: that abusers get help to change or that they are punished?
- How do you think the abusers feel about their behaviour?
- If violence in families could be stopped by changing attitudes, would that affect attitudes to war and other forms of social violence?

List all the ways that you know of how children are protected from abuse. Include in your list the voluntary agencies that work to protect children and help their parents. Also list the ways that children who have been abused can be helped to get over the experience.

Examine the part that education has to play in the prevention of child abuse. Remember that children and adults can be educated both formally and informally.

Present your ideas to others in a way that has

some impact, that is, in a way that other people will take notice of.

Further work could include one of the following:

1. Watch a video designed to help young children avoid sexual abuse. Decide whether you would have benefited from seeing it as a child.
2. List the ways that children can be encouraged to behave without resorting to smacking them.
3. Role-play with a partner the parents of a family of three children. The mother loves her partner very much, but does not like the way he controls the children. One of you take the part of the mother and one the father.
4. Invent a new way of fund-raising for a children's charity of your choice.

9 Is it difficult to bring up children? ◈◈

> **What you should learn**
>
> - That becoming a parent can change your life
> - That job descriptions issued by employers can help you decide whether you could do the job or not
> - Training is not supplied for the job of being a parent
> - Legal documents are difficult to understand
>
> **What you will need**
>
> A double lesson   Word-processors would be
> Paper   useful, if available
> Pen/pencil

Read carefully what these parents of young children have said:

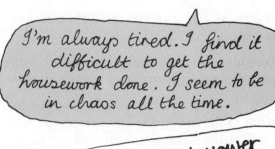

I'm always tired. I find it difficult to get the housework done. I seem to be in chaos all the time.

When I first brought my daughter home from the hospital, I was so happy. Six months later I'm a wreck.

I didn't realize what a mess children make.

I didn't appreciate what my parents did for me until I had kids of my own.

If only they didn't argue so much.

We really need a bigger home. If I had one I'd make one of the rooms a child-free zone.

It was great when they were little but now they're in their teens I can't cope with their moods

We can't afford any of the things we used to take for granted. I'd love a night out on the town.

I'm fascinated with how quickly children grow up. They keep me busy, but make me feel young.

It's better now that Adam goes to school and Clare goes to playgroup a couple of mornings a week. I get a bit of time for myself.

The older I get the less patience I have for their bad behaviour.

In groups, list some of the difficulties of parenting.

Consider the following: If it is such difficult job, why do so many people take it on?

How do people know how to be a parent? What skills are needed to do the job well? Look at the advertisement and job description for a Nursery Assistant in the London Borough of Walford.

Nursery Assistant

To help nursery teacher in our purpose-built provision for 3–5 year olds. Experience in a school/group setting essential, NNEB preferred. We are hoping to appoint a mature person to this post. A First-Aid qualification would be an advantage.

Hours 8.30 am – 4.30 pm.

Salary £5,160 – £5934 dependent on age and qualifications.

Application form and further details from:
The Headteacher,
Allbrights Infants School,
Chesterfield Drive,
Walford.

Walford is an Equal Opportunity employer. Applications are considered regardless of disability, sex, race, age, marital status and sexual orientation. We would particularly welcome applicants from the ethnic community this authority serves.

Applicants selected for interview will be invited to visit the school.

JOB TITLE:. Nursery Assistant

LOCATION:. Allbrights Infant School

JOB DESCRIPTION

Main duties

1   To assist the nursery teacher with the care and education of the children who attend the nursery class.
2   To deputise for the teacher on the few occasions she has to leave the class.

Job activities

1   Preparing the learning activity materials.
2   Arranging the room at the start of the session.
3   Helping to supervise the children both in the classroom and in the outside playspace.
4   Completing the sessional register
5   Tidying up the classroom at the end of each session.
6   Reporting to the teacher any broken or dangerous play materials.
7   Supervising the care of the classroom animals.
8   Preparing and distributing the mid-session refreshments.
9   Attending training sessions as required.
10 Performing any other tasks that the nursery teacher requires.

Using a word-processor if you have one or writing by hand, **write** a realistic job description for a parent. Once you have completed the job description you could make an advertisement for that job.

Read the following extract. This is the section entitled CHILDREN from a legal contract which a couple drew up, with the help of a sympathetic lawyer, before their marriage to protect their individual rights and define their major responsibilities to each other.

---

a We agree that as we are of different religions, any child of this marriage may choose their own religion once they have reached the age of 16 years. Until that time any children shall be brought up in the Jewish faith.

b We agree to share equally the responsibilities of parenthood be those physical, emotional or financial. We recognise that there may be times and situations when one or other of us is under more pressure at work or in our personal life, and at such times the least pressurised will naturally bear more of the burden. However, it is our intention that the load is equalised over the long term, neither one of us having the right to claim freedom from these responsibilities.

c We agree that our children will be given equal opportunities regardless of their sex.

d We agree that the equal responsibility for the financial support of our children shall continue until the child has attained independent status or the age of 24 years whichever is the soonest. We also agree to continue this support regardless of our marital status at that time.

e Our children will be registered and known under the surname of our unmarried names hyphenated in alphabetical order, that is Cohen-Taylor.

f If the marriage does not result in any children and an adoption of a child or children takes place, this contract shall equally apply to them.

g We agree that Ruth has the right to conceive a child of John's by the time she is 30 years old. If a medical opinion finds John to be sterile, Ruth has the right to conceive a child by other means.

h We agree that should we fail to agree on any major decision needed to fulfil our parental responsibilities a third party, mutually agreed upon, should be asked to negotiate with us a satisfactory resolution.

Have another look at your job description. Is it suitable for either parent? Do you need to alter the wording so that it does apply to either the mother or the father?

Display your final work and discuss any differences between yours and others.

Choose a further idea to develop:
1 Write a contract between a teenager and a parent or parents. Your contract should set out clearly how both should act towards the other.
2 Suggest some ways in which parents could be supported in doing the job of bringing up a family.
3 Design a programme of learning for parents-to-be that could be offered as an evening class by your local authority.
4 Design and make a rough prototype of a game that would help the players develop some of the skills and attitudes needed for the job of parenting.

10 Whose job is it to look after the welfare of children? ◇◇

What you should learn

- How to plan and organise a visit to your class/group
- How to welcome a stranger and look after her/his needs
- How to use best the expertise of a visitor

What you will need

Time to plan
Time for the visitors to come to your school or college
Use of telephone
Letter paper/envelopes/stamps
Paper
Pen/pencil

In a group, **generate** a list of people whose job it is to look after the welfare of children. Remember that the welfare of children can be concerned with health, education, the law, social policy, government, morals, etc. Your group should **choose** someone they would like to talk to about their job and its role in the welfare of children. Each group should choose a different one to interview. You may need to negotiate your choice with your teacher and the other groups.

Plan the visit in detail. You will need to decide when the visitor should come and for how long. You will need to invite the visitor; this can be done by telephone with a letter of confirmation to follow. You may need to give the visitor some travelling instructions so that they can find the place easily. You will need to plan how you are going to use the visitor's expertise to help you with your studies. How can you get a good discussion going with the visitor? Will the visitor need to know what you are going to ask her/him? How are you going to record the information you gain from having the visitor come? Will you want to write a letter of thanks to the visitor after the visit?

An important part of this work will be to share with the rest of your class what you have found out. There are many ways of doing this. One way would be for each group to write a report about the role of the person they meet. The reports could then be stored together and be built up over the years into a very useful resource for future investigations.

Further work you could do:

1 Write a list of the ways that people can put pressure on local or central government to improve the community welfare of children.
2 Find out what jobs are available in the community where you can work with children. You could find out what qualifications are needed for each one and what salary range is offered for such work.
3 How can people in this country help with the improved welfare of children who live in poverty in other countries? Record your ideas.
4 Redesign the logo of any children's charity. You will need to have reasons for the changes you make.

11 Who should look after these children?

What you should learn

- How to deal with a lot of information
- To analyse a problem needing a solution
- To share a workload

What you will need

Two double lessons	Pen/pencil
Large paper	Dictionary
Markers	A range of materials for
Paper	presenting feedback to the class

Please note: There may be people in your group who have been or are being cared for by someone other than their parents. Please remember that students in this position might find this an emotional topic. However, they will be able to contribute much to the discussion and should be listened to very carefully.

Read all the documents that follow. They are all case conference reports about the Morris twins. It might be a good idea if you **share** this task between you, working as individuals or in parts or taking turns to read to each other.

The documents are:
- Report by Hospital Social Worker
- Report by Maternity Ward Sister
- Report by Mary Morris's GP
- Report from Social Worker, Gravesend District
- Police Report.

Make a chart with all the information you gather from the reports. Remember to distinguish the facts from the opinion.

Decide the solutions to the following:
1 Should Mary's parents be allowed to foster the twins?
2 What alternatives should be considered?
3 Is there extra information that could be gathered before decisions can be made? If so, what should happen to the twins whilst that is happening?

Communicate your group's judgements to the whole class. Choose a way of doing this that will use the talents of the people in your group.

Report by Hospital Social Worker

I met Mary Morris on one occasion. It was the seventh day after her Caesarian section operation. She appeared to be an intelligent young woman and was obviously proud of her two babies. She was reticent about disclosing much of her personal life. She did tell me that she had given false details of her address when she was admitted into the hospital. She was not prepared to rectify that. She said that she was rather worried about managing to look after the twin girls and said she wanted time to think about what she should do. We arranged to meet again on 21.3.89 at 3.00 pm. This time she was to come to my office which would be a more private place to meet than the ward. I felt sure she would be more open about her circumstances once she had considered her position. When she didn't keep her appointment, I telephoned the ward sister who informed me that Mary had left the ward, taking her few possessions with her She had not taken the twins with her.

On the 22nd March, Mrs Stephanie Morris and I had a long discussion about her daughter. It appears that Mary left home four days before her sixteenth birthday and apart from one Christmas card, postmarked Nottingham, she had had no news of how her daughter was. Mary is an only child and her father, a Mr Frederick Morris, had taken her disappearance very badly. He has been under treatment for depression ever since and had been laid off work after a very long period of sick leave. Mrs Morris has a part-time job as a receptionist at a hairdresser and she says that the family finances are adequate. They own their own home, a semi-detached three-bedroom house on a new estate in Gravesend, Kent. She looked well dressed and is obviously a car-owner as she explained that she had driven to the station to come to this hospital.

Her main concern seemed to be for the twins, rather than for her daughter who she seems to have given up as a lost cause. She asked whether the babies had been tested for HIV as she was sure her daughter had been having 'a high old time'. She told me that she had come to collect the babies as it was surely her right as their grandmother. I explained that we were hoping to locate her daughter through the police and that, for the present, the twins would remain in the care of the nurses on the maternity ward. She then became quite abusive and left in a temper. I tried to telephone her on the following day. She refused to have any more dealings with me, having, she said, put the matter in the hands of a solicitor.

Report by Ward Sister – Maternity Ward, Getwell Hospital, London

On 12.3.89, Mary Morris aged 17 years 1 month was admitted in labour to this ward. She was hazy about the dates of her last menstrual period, but appeared on examination to be at full-term of her pregnancy. She had not sought any antenatal care. Apart from signs of slight maternal malnutrition, resulting in a degree of anaemia, the mother was relatively healthy. Further examination revealed her to be carrying twins. After eight hours of labour a decision was made to prepare her for Caesarian section. Twin girls were delivered safely. The older girl weighed 2.9kg, the younger 2.8kg. After the birth Mary appeared to be coping with the postoperative discomfort but was rather weepy. She opted to bottle feed her babies and by the eighth day after birth they had regained their birthweight. The hospital social worker was asked to discuss with Ms Morris the future welfare of the children. Ms Morris had only one visitor during her stay in hospital. A young man visited her three times. On the ninth day, just after she had been informed that she would be discharged with the twins on the following day, Ms Morris dressed and disappeared from the ward leaving the twins behind. After establishing that she had indeed left the hospital, her next of kin, her mother, a Mrs Stephanie Morris, was informed. Her mother had not known that her daughter was pregnant. The grandmother did show great concern for the twins and on the following day arrived on the ward ready to take them home. I asked her to talk with the hospital social worker which she did.

At a meeting here at the hospital it was decided that we request the area social services team to take over the responsibility for the twins' welfare. We would appreciate an early response to this problem as we do not really have the resources to care for the twins in this maternity hospital.

Report by Mary Morris's GP in Gravesend

I knew Mary Morris from 14.2.72 – 12.12.87. I last saw her when she consulted me for contraceptive advice. I explained to her at the time that I did not prescribe contraceptives and that the local Family Planning Association held a clinic for young people every Tuesday evening at the Fernhead Road Centre. I suggested she attend there as soon as possible. She appeared to be in good health at that time apart from being a little overweight. I did notice, however, that the clothes she wore were hardly warm enough on such a bitterly cold day. I remember she told me that fashion was far more important to her than feeling warm. I did ask her whether she had talked to her parents about the need for contraceptives and suggested she did so before she went to the clinic in Fernhead Road. I got the impression that she had no intention of doing so in spite of her agreeing with me the need for their support. Prior to that occasion I had only treated Mary for the usual coughs, colds and childhood infectious diseases.

Report by Social Worker, Area 3, Gravesend

I visited Mrs Stephanie Morris and Mr Frederick Morris at their home in Gravesend. I understand that my view is required as to whether the grandparents would be suitable foster parents for twins born to their daughter Mary.

The Morris house is tidy, precisely organised, clean and bright. The gardens front and back are small but well tended. Mrs Morris is obviously very houseproud and seems to do all the work involved in the house and garden as well as manage a part-time job. Mr Morris explained, whilst Mrs Morris was out of the room preparing some tea, that his wife had become obsessed with the appearance of their home since she spent a month in prison as a result of an episode of shop-lifting. He felt she was ashamed of that bad period in her life and used the home to get rid of the feelings she had about it. He told me that he finds life difficult having to live up to this high standard while she is out doing her job. When Mrs Morris rejoined us we had tea together whilst I completed our standard questionnaire. From the information I gathered, there is no question that there is enough room, money and goodwill for the twins to be fostered by these grandparents. Both are regular churchgoers. Mr Morris helps with the local Scouts and Mrs Morris is a Sunday School teacher. Their kitchen includes both washing and tumble-dryer machines. They would be prepared to fill in the small pond in the back garden, realising that this could be hazardous for young children.

My only anxieties are the history of shop-lifting, caused, in the husband's opinion, by the anxiety about the daughter, Mary. I also have my doubts in relation to the obsessive tidiness of the home, the history of depression in the grandfather and the unequal partnership with regard to the chores. I wonder whether having two young children to care for would improve or worsen this situation? It is difficult to say without much further counselling of both grandparents.

Police Report Re: Mary Morris

We have been unable to find this young woman. The address given to us by the hospital, 19 Faversham Court, End Well Road, Nottingham, has been visited by the local police. She apparently did live there but left in September 1988 leaving no forwarding address. The present occupiers have never met her and the immediate neighbours only remember her for the very loud music she constantly played. We are continuing to use the normal channels in order to locate her for you, but doubt whether she will be located in the near future.

Further work you could do:
1 Talk to someone who fosters children on a short-term basis. Find out what it feels like to give up children once you've started to get fond of them.
2 Make sure you know the difference between fostering and adoption. If you were a child in need of a home, which would you prefer? Write short notes.
3 Could anything have been done at the hospital to prevent Mary leaving her children? Record your ideas any way you wish.
4 Role-play with a friend Mary and her boyfriend discussing what she had done. One of you be Mary and the other her boyfriend Tim.

12 Should children work? ◈◈

Look at the following children:

Making kerbstones

Sweeping chimneys

■ LINDSAY SUTHERLAND, aged 10, from Gravesend, Kent.

"Lindsay will do anything for me—for anyone," says disabled Pat Sutherland of her very special 10-year-old granddaughter.

"She dresses me, gets my drugs, cooks, washes and does the ironing. She's looked after me since she was four or five—and she never complains."

Lindsay, who lives with her mother and grandmother, often spends her weekends with a 75-year-old neighbour who's recovering from cancer—keeping her company and doing her shopping. "She really loves Lindsay," says a proud Pat.

When she's not looking after her grandmother, Lindsay can be found collecting for charity. "She's helped collect over £2,000 for charity," says Pat. "She thinks nothing of standing outside with a collecting tin all day."

She also looks after two disabled friends at school. "I get their dinner for them and I help them if they get stuck," says Lindsay.

"It seems to be inbuilt in her," says Lindsay's mum Andrea. "Even when she's ill herself she never grumbles.

"A couple of years ago she was in the kitchen cooking breakfast for my mum and dad—it was their wedding anniversary—and a cupboard fell on her.

"Her hand was cut open to the bone and the doctor said he'd never seen anything like it. But she didn't make any fuss—her main concern was that she didn't want to have to miss her dancing lesson that night!"

"I want to be a dancer," says Lindsay, an astonishingly mature child for her age. "But if I can't be a dancer, I'll be a nurse. I want to be able to carry on helping other people as much as I can."

Interior decorating

Acting on television

Picking fruit on a farm

Doing the laundry

Modelling clothes

Decide which ones are working, which ones are playing and which ones are helping. Once you have done that decide what your group means by working, playing and helping.

Study the information about the laws relating to children working and the extract from the United Nations Convention on the Rights of the Child.

Children working and the law

1   Children are protected from exploitation in the United Kingdom by laws which make it illegal for employers to employ children under a certain age.
2   Children are only allowed to work in certain jobs that are considered safe for them to do so.
3   Children are not allowed to work full-time as they are legally bound to attend school.
4   Weekend and evening work for children is limited to a restricted number of hours. Children are not allowed to work at night.
5   Children who want to work before or after school or at the weekend must have both their parents' and their school's permission to do so. A special form has to be completed by the child, the parent/s and the headteacher and the employer before the child may start work.

As a group **discuss**:
● Whether the regulations about children working in the United Kingdom are effective or not. Are children being exploited by employers?
● What could be done to make the rules work better?
● Should children help adults? What are the advantages of children being encouraged to help adults? What might be the problems if children are expected to help too much? Think of these issues from the points of view of the children and of the adults.

Decide what is the difference between working and being given money to help.

Use the resources you have available to help you decide at what age children could be expected to help by doing the tasks listed in the chart opposite. Fill in a copy of the chart.

Article 18

1 The States Parties to the present Convention recognize the right of the child to be protected from economic exploitation and from performing any work that is likely to be hazardous or interfere with the child's education, or be harmful to the child's health or physical, mental, spiritual, moral or social development.
2 The States Parties to the present Convention shall take legislative and administrative measures to ensure the implementation of this article. To this end, and having regard to the relevant provisions of other international instruments, the States Parties shall in particular:
(a) provide for a minimum age or minimum ages for admission into employment;
(b) provide for appropriate regulation of hours and conditions of employment; and,
(c) provide for appropriate penalties or other sanctions to ensure the effective enforcement of this article.
Extract from the United Nation's Convention on the Rights of the Child.

If you have time you may also like to consider:

1   Why, in spite of the laws, some children in the United Kingdom still work illegally?
2   Who in the United Kingdom is responsible for monitoring the position of children with regard to work?
3   Where could children go for help if they felt they were being exploited by an employer?
4   How can adults help children worldwide who are being made to work?

Task	The youngest age at which a child could be expected to do this	Why that age?
Wash up		
Clean shoes		
Make own bed		
Clear table		
Ironing		
Lay table		
Tidy bedroom		
Clean car		
Mow lawn		
Do washing at launderette		
Get shopping		
Take messages to neighbours		
Clean floors		
Contribute to family finance		
Buy own clothes		
Help in family business		

13 What are the hazards? ◇

Choose any one of the places drawn in the picture below and investigate the hazards to children that it might pose.

You can **consider** such issues as safety, protection, health, exploitation and pollution.

You could also consider physical, intellectual, social, economic, historical, moral, commercial and legal influences.

You can use primary and or secondary sources of information.

Communicate the results of your investigation in any way you choose. For those of you who are going to do examinations that require you to do an investigation this would be a chance to practice writing a formal report. You could then get some feedback from your teacher and fellow students about how you could improve your reporting style. On page xx there is an assignment that should help you with writing a formal report.

You could develop your ideas by doing one of the following:

1 Design a game that would help children to avoid one or more of the hazards you have found out about.

2 Write a puppet play in which a child avoids a hazard.
3 Share your findings with someone else who chose to investigate the same place as yourself. Compare your approach to the task, the sources of information that you used and your conclusions.
4 Compose an advertising jingle to warn adults of a particular hazard to children. Record this on tape. You might need to persuade a performing musician to help you.

14 Should children be the targets of commercial advertising? ◇

Read the advertisement from a magazine published in 1931.

Watch a TV advertisement for a toy or set of toys. **Note** the time of day it was shown, what was the content of the advertisement and whether it is repeated over a period of a week or so. If you have a video recorder it would be a good idea to **record** it so that you can analyse it carefully.

- Decide what is similar about the two advertisements.
- Decide what is different.
- Consider the effect of social change over the last 50–60 years.
- Consider the following factors:
  Cost
  Type of toy
  Materials used in its construction
  Style of advertisements
  Effect of the advertisements
  Who are the advertisements targeted at?
  The advertising standards

Investigate what parents think about TV advertising of toys and games for children.

Further work you could do:
1 Add any standards to the list that you think should be there, or alter any you think are wrong. Give your reasons. Discuss your list with others who have attempted this task. If you feel that together you have a particularly valid point, you could communicate the idea direct to CAP. Their address is on p. xx.
2 Look at advertisements for toys and games in magazines, newspapers, TV and identify any that you think do not comply with the advertising standards.
3 With another student, role-play a parent explaining to a small child that they cannot afford to buy a toy the child has set her/his heart on.
4 Investigate just how influential TV advertising of toys is on children's requests/hopes for Christmas presents and the possible implications for families.

Section C.X Children

1.1   Direct appeals or exhortations to buy should not be made to children unless the product advertised is one likely to be of interest to them and one which they could reasonably be expected to afford for themselves.

1.2   Advertisements should not encourage children to make themselves a nuisance to their parents, or anyone else, with the aim of pursuading them to buy an advertised product.

1.3   No advertisement should cause children to believe that they will be inferior to other children, or unpopular with them, if they do not buy a particular product, or have it bought for them.

1.4   No advertisement for a commercial product should suggest to children that, if they do not buy it and encourage others to do so, they will be failing in their duty or lacking in loyalty.

1.5   Advertisements addressed to children should make it easy for a child to judge the true size of a product (preferably by showing it in relation to some common object) and should take care to avoid any confusion between the characteristics of real-life articles and toy copies of them.

1.6   Where the results obtainable by the use of a product are shown, these should not exaggerate what is attainable by an ordinary child.

1.7   Advertisements addressed to children should, wherever possible, give the price of the advertised product.

1.8   No advertisement, especially one offering a product for supply by mail order, should appear in a medium directed at children if, for whatever reason, that product is unsuitable for purchase or use by the children who are likely to see the advertisement.

Safety

2.1   Special care should be taken to avoid the likelihood of children copying any practices which are either inherently unsafe, or likely to become unsafe when engaged in by children. The following paragraphs highlight some particular danger areas in advertisements likely to appeal to children.

2.2   No advertisement, particularly for a collecting scheme, should encourage children to enter strange places or to converse with strangers in an effort to collect coupons, wrappers, labels and the like.

2.3   Children should not appear to be unattended in street scenes unless they are obviously old enough to be responsible for their own safety; they should not be shown playing in the road, unless it is clearly shown to be a play-street or other safe area; they should not be shown stepping carelessly off the pavement or crossing the road without due care; in busy street scenes they should be seen to use the zebra crossings when crossing the road; and otherwise they should be seen in general to behave, as pedestrians or cyclists, in accordance with the Highway Code.

2.4   **1.** Children should not be seen behaving dangerously, e.g. leaning far out of windows, stading on the parapets of bridges or climbing without adequate supervision or protection.

       2. Small children should not be shown climbing up to high shelves or reaching up to take things from above their heads.

2.5   Medicines, disinfectants, antiseptics and caustic substances should not be shown within reach of children without close parental supervision, nor should unsupervised children be shown using these products in any way.

2.6   Children should not be shown using matches or gas, paraffin, petrol or any mechanical or electrical appliance which could lead to their suffering burns, electrical shock or other injury.

2.7   Children should not be shown driving or riding on agricultural machines (including tractor-drawn carts or implements), so as to encourage contravention of the Agriculture (Avoidance of Accidents to Children Regulations) 1958 SI 361.

2.8   An open fire should have a fireguard clearly visible when a child is included in the scene.

15 How can young children's health be ensured? ◇

Parents, health workers, local government and central government all have roles to play in the maintenance of children's health. **Investigate** one of those roles. Use primary and/or secondary sources.

The key issues are:
- What do we mean by health?

> 'Health is a state of complete physical, mental and social well-being, not merely the absence of disease and infirmity.'
> *World Health Organisation Definition*

- Is health provision an environmental issue?
- Is good health a personal or community responsibility?

If you find you are stuck on getting started by yourself, try first to list all the factors you think could be relevant.

Identify points you need to clarify.

Group factors together that seem to be linked.

Decide if you need to gather any specific information.

An example

You are investigating the role of a young child in keeping him or herself healthy. We'll consider a 6-year-old. List all the relevant factors:
(a) Clean own teeth
(b) Wash hands after going to lavatory
(c) Drink plenty of water
(d) Not add salt to food at the table
(e) Wash self/nails/hair/body
(f) Brush and comb hair
(g) Make friends
(h) Develop interests that they really enjoy.

Identify points you need to clarify:
  Does combing the hair keep it healthy?
  Are lonely children unhealthy?

Can six-year-olds wash themselves and their hair?

Group factors that seem to be linked:
(a), (b), (e), (f)   Cleanliness/hygiene
(c), (d)   Dietary factors they could be taught to control themselves.
(g), (h)   Social/emotional development.

Decide whether you need to gather any specific information:

1   What's the best way to teach children to clean their teeth – the advice seems to vary in different books/leaflets?
2   Do children of this age understand the health hazard of not washing their hands after using the lavatory? Do adults?
3   Do children have a chance to:
    (a) Learn about healthy eating?
    (b) Use that knowledge. Or is it always in the control of the adults who care for her/him? For example, is extra salt put on the table in primary schools at lunchtime?
    (c) Develop interests that they really enjoy? Is that limited by the home environment, parental expectations, availability of time and money?

If you get this far you've developed the ideas you need for an investigation. All you need to do is decide how you can find out that specific information. Remember that people, adults and children, can be a very good source of information.

If you find yourself with time to spare on this assignment, you could do one of the following:

1   Make a story book that would help a child to understand a simple health message.
2   Write a pamphlet to be distributed in your community. The pamphlet should highlight the dangers of a particularly unhealthy habit; eg, spitting.
3   Design a poster that would help parents understand how they can help to keep their child healthy.
4   Design an interview schedule that could be used to make a radio programme concerning child health.

Investigational homeworks

1 **Look** carefully at the photograph. List all the visual clues that tell you that this photograph is an old one. Can you deduce how old it is? Write a short account of what a child's life was like in those days. You may have to visit the library for some information.

2 **Compare** a book intended for a child with one intended for an adult. Find at least *five* major differences and *five* major similarities. You will probably find more than that. Make lists of what you discover.

3 **Design** a questionnaire to find out what different generations feel about discipline in childhood.

4 **Draw** a diagram that depicts your family. You may have to ask members of your family for some of the information you need to be able to do this.

5 **Make** a plaything for a two-year-old. The plaything should cost less than 20p to produce. Write notes on why you chose to make the plaything you did.

6 **Visit** the children's section of a local library.

Talk to at least one parent about why they use the children's library and how they decide what to borrow.

Write a short but detailed account of what you find out.

7 In a small research survey carried out in 1988, parents, teachers, adults without children and adolescents were asked to identify the five qualities most needed for parenthood. The only quality agreed on by all four groups was the need for a 'sense of humour'.

Suggest reasons why these people thought that parents needed a sense of humour. How do children develop a sense of humour? Is a sense of humour encouraged at your school? Write down which activities, lessons and people have helped to develop your sense of humour.

8 **Find out** where is the
(a) nearest playgroup
(b) nearest open space
(c) nearest infant school
in relation to your home. Draw a simple street map showing where these places are. How long would it take to walk to each? What problems might a parent have travelling to them with a child walking alongside a baby in a buggy?

9 **Visit** a local playspace for children. Examine the facilities in a critical way. Write a brief report for your local council describing its present state and the implications for safety. Recommend what could be done to improve the site. You may get a chance to talk to parents and children in order to get their views as well.

10 **Read** the following letter to a magazine with the reply from their 'agony aunt':

Not in front of the children

My husband and I have our fair share of disagreements, like every other "happily married" couple, I suppose. The problem, if there is one, is that my husband refuses to discuss things in front of our children if we might disagree as he says it would only distress them. So it usually ends up with us discussing anything difficult very late at night when I'm too tired to think straight, and am ratty, and I think this makes our disagreements worse than they need be.

■ Providing the children don't feel they live in the middle of a permanent battleground, I think it can be quite healthy for them to witness disagreements aired and resolved. That is education for them about real life. If they never see an argument or see that people can make up afterwards they may come to believe that anger should never be expressed and that "happy" families don't disagree and hence have very unrealistic ideas of marital life.

Write down if you agree with the reply, giving your reasons. Comment upon any improvements you could make to the reply. Decide why you think people write to 'agony aunts' about their problems.

11 An infant schoolteacher was doing a project with her pupils called 'What happens in the early morning?'. She was going to use the project to teach the children about time, travel, people who start work when others are still asleep, people who came home from working during the night, and many other ideas that young children do not understand. To start them off thinking about the early morning, she asked them to draw a picture of something that happened in their home before school started.

One 5-year-old drew a picture and, as was the custom, asked her teacher to write underneath. 'This is Daddy. He is opening the front door. He is picking up the milk and pissing the cat.' The teacher felt rather embarassed about the 'pissing' so asked the child, 'What does he do to the cat?' 'He says *pss-pss-pss*,' said the child, 'he doesn't like them walking on his flowers.'

Write your own example of a child's conversation where the child has used some rather strange language. Interpret what you think they were trying to say.

12 Read the following newspaper article.

CHILD AT LAST AFTER ADOPTING TWO

Kid stuff: Sue with Katie, husband Steve and Ben and Elizabeth

And baby makes three in our happiest family

PROUD mother Sue Miller cuddled her own one-in-a- million baby yesterday—after spending £12,000 to adopt two OTHER babies.

Doctors told hairdresser Sue, 31, to give up the idea of becoming a mother after suffering a stillbirth and an ectopic pregnancy.

So Sue and her husband Stephen, 36, who runs a chain of hairdressing salons, decided to adopt.

They paid £12,000 arranging to adopt a boy and a girl born to poor maids who could not afford to keep them in strife-torn El Savador.

But as the adoption was just being finalised on their second child, Sue found that she was pregnant with daughter Katie.

Yesterday at home in Heather Hills, Stockton Brook, Stoke on Trent, Sue said: "It was a miracle."

The couple adopted Ben, now 22 months, when he was 10 weeks and Elizabeth, now seven months, when she was seven weeks.

Sue said: "Now, with three children around the house, I really do have my hands full—and I'm thrilled to bits."

Husband Stephen said: "Adopting Ben and Elizabeth cost us £12,000 mainly on solicitors' fees and travel to El Salvador. We did not pay anything for the babies.

"Of course, we have no regrets over the adoptions. We never believed we would have a child of our own."

Do some investigating about adoption.

(a) Is it normally an expensive procedure?

(b) Why would a couple need to find a child all the way from El Salvador?

(c) How should these parents explain to their children the different circumstances that made their family grow?

13 Read the following newspaper cutting:

(a) What reasons might Ben's mother have to prefer employing a young man to look after her son whilst she is at work?

(b) Why is it often the case that women rather than men are in jobs that involve the care and education of young children? Think about why this is so in these times when equal opportunity is considered important.

TEARS AS BEN'S FRIEND IS KICKED OUT

Homeward bound: Male au pair Hakan says goodbye to Ben

Farewell, au pair pal!

AU PAIR Hakan Larsson said a tearful farewell yesterday to the little boy he had come to Britain to look after, when immigration officials threw him out of the country.

Eight-year-old Ben Oberman burst into tears as his Swedish friend left from Heathrow Airport after just a week here.

Officials had ordered Hakan, who comes from Gothenberg, to leave after insisting there was no such thing as a male au pair.

Ben's mum, author Wendy Oberman, 45, had invited Hakan to Britain to look after her son while she worked on her writing.

Now she has written to MPs Rosie Barnes and Sir Hugh Rossi to complain about the immigration ruling.

14 Mary's grandparents arranged a ninth birthday celebration for her. They took her and one friend, a boy of 8 years, and Mary's parents to a restaurant in the evening for a meal. Mary wore a shiny, mini-skirted dress and high-heeled shoes. When asked what she wanted to drink with her meal, Mary asked for and got the alcoholic drink she wanted.

Do you think that the celebration was a suitable one? Give your reasons. Can you think of a better way for a child to be given a treat on her ninth birthday? Write down what you think.

15 According to the birth statistics of 1987, fewer couples are worried now about having a baby before marriage. Almost 1 in 4 children, that is 430 a day in the United Kingdom, are born outside marriage. Half of the 158,000 illegitimate babies were, however, born to couples living together in stable relationships.

(a) **Use this information** to draw a histogram showing the comparison between the numbers of children born to married couples, couples within a stable relationship and to single parents.
(b) What do you feel about these statistics?
(c) Does the type of family they are born into affect the children? Give reasons for your answer.

16 Nursery rhymes are traditionally read and sung to young children. Many of them seem nonsensical. Children usually like learning them and are proud to be able, at quite an early age, to remember them.

Can you **remember** the ones you learned as a child?

Find out, if you don't know already, what 'Ring-a-ring-a-roses' and 'Georgy Porgy' were historically all about.

Invent a new nursery rhyme using a tragedy, or political or social comment relevant to today's world.

17 There are several comics published for the pre-school child. Choose a picture story from one of these comics and analyse the messages being conveyed to the children. Examine both the pictures and the writing when doing this task.

18 **Watch** a TV programme intended for young children. Describe its format and evaluate its usefulness in terms of children's learning, in particular, with language development. If you have a video recorder it would be sensible to record the programme so that you can view it more than once in order to analyse it carefully.

19 There is an old saying 'Early to bed, early to rise makes a man healthy, wealthy and wise'. **Investigate** whether this is true for children.

20 An infant school headteacher recommends that before children start primary school they ought to be able to do the following by themselves:

dress and undress;

use the toilet properly;

use a handkerchief efficiently to blow their noses.

(a) Why do you think the headteacher makes these recommendations?
(b) Could you add to the list?
(c) Which ones might prove difficult for a parent to achieve? Say why. If you wanted to, you could **make a booklet**, entitled 'Getting Ready for School', with all your recommendations, giving the reasons behind them. The booklet would be for parents with children soon to be starting school.

How do you get a good investigational idea of your own?

Some examination syllabuses require you to think of your own idea for an investigation. This part of the book is for those of you who might find it difficult to get an idea that is suited to your circumstances. It can be very frustrating watching other students progressing with their chosen ideas, whilst you are still unclear about what you should do. These are a few ways that can be tried to help you get started.

1 Keeping track of ideas as they happen

Have a page in your coursework file ready for you to note down, as the course progresses, anything that you:

- Find difficult to believe
- Contradicts your own experience
- Conflicts with information you've gained from other sources
- Are surprised about
- Have found extremely interesting
- Are worried about.

By the time you are asked to start developing ideas for an individual investigation you should have some starting points already. You'll then need to go through the ideas you've noted and choose the best one to develop into an investigation.

Example

Suppose you had noted two linked things that you found extremely interesting. These were:

(a) that pre-conceptual health clinics now operate in some parts of the United Kingdom. At these clinics, experts recommend both partners to at least reduce their alcohol consumption *before* they conceive a child;

(b) that babies can be born with a medical condition called foetal-alcohol syndrome if the mother drinks too much alcohol during her pregnancy;

(c) that in the newspaper and on TV you learned that in the USA a woman was suing a whisky manufacturing company because they had not printed a warning on their product about the danger to unborn children. She had drunk $\frac{1}{2} - \frac{2}{3}$ of a bottle every day of the pregnancy and had given birth to a child with the syndrome.

You could decide to ask people their opinions about whose fault it was, the mother's or the whisky company's. Or was it the government for not issuing health warnings to the general public? Or you could decide to find out whether people in this country know about the dangers of alcohol consumption to the unborn child. Or you could find out whether doctors warn their patients about the dangers of alcohol consumption prior to and during pregnancy. Or you could find out what should in general be avoided during pregnancy in order to protect the health of the unborn child.

2 Using your outside school/college interests

Interests that you have that are connected with childhood

This is usually a very successful way of generating an idea for an investigation. Anything that you are already involved with will make it more interesting to do and you will be able to demonstrate that you know what you are talking about.

All you have to do is to note everything you do in your home and community life that is connected with children.

Example

John noted his child-related interests as a spider chart:

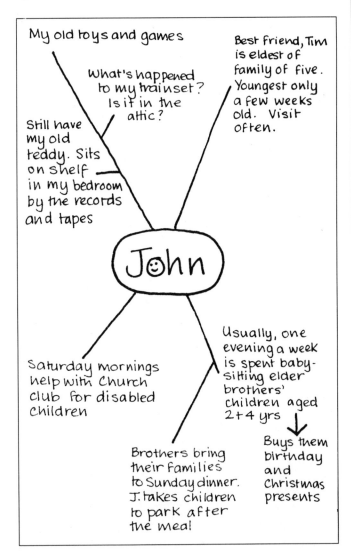

So John could investigate many aspects of babysitting; how to choose presents suitable for the developmental stage his niece and nephew are at; how to help children learn whilst walking in the park; whether or not all children have special comfort toys or what makes one soft toy become a particular favourite. He could interview his best friend's mother to find out if it is hard to manage a large family that includes a newly-born baby or he could use his experience of helping disabled children to develop an investigation.

Interests you have that do not seem to be related to children

Sometimes, interests and activities you are involved with can have some child connections that could make fascinating investigations.

Example

It is John again.

> **What I spend my time on** (not homework)
> ✓ Watching TV
>   Delivering papers
>   Swimming and life-saving
> ✓ Holidays in the sun with my family
>   Discos
> ✓ Football (watching not playing)
>   Helping my father to decorate house
>   Collecting first-day covers
> ✓ Reading Science fiction

Make your own list. Choose two or three of your favourite interests/activities to explore ideas.

John chose the ones he ticked on his list. Then he started to think about those things with young children in mind. He came up with many ideas:

Do children watch too much TV? Or programmes that frighten them? How much time on TV is devoted to programmes designed for the pre-school child? How do parents keep young children occupied on a flight to a holiday abroad? What do parents do with young children in the summer if they can not afford holidays? Should young children go to football matches? Is it too crowded and dangerous for them? How do children's tastes in books change as they get older?

3 Seeing an idea in a book, but adapting it to make it your own idea

A book like this one is full of ideas that you could develop in your own way.

Example

Look at page 47, Homework no. 18.

Could you take this idea further?

You could, for instance, buy a comic intended to be suitable for a pre-school child, analyse its total content, test the material with young children and evaluate it, making decisions about what is suitable for that age group and what is not. A useful way of demonstrating its problems would be to devise a more suitable alternative, saying why you thought so.

Look at page 47, Homework no. 17.

It would be interesting to interview children about what they thought nursery rhymes mean. Children strive to make sense of their world and they would probably have quite interesting answers to your questions.

4 Sorting out the topics of interest

Usually on any course of study different topics interest different students. To work out what your favourite topics have been, first write down on small pieces of paper all the topics about children you have studied. You can then sort those topics into three piles: very interesting; interesting; and not so interesting.

Take your 'very interesting' pile and list all the parts of each topic you really enjoyed. Sort all those parts of topics into three piles again as before. You should, by now, be finding a

specific area of interest that could give you an idea to investigate.

Example

Jane did this sorting exercise and found herself left with a pile of pieces of paper with these part-topics written on them:

Designing a toy	
Play objects that are not sold as toys	} from a PLAY topic
Contraceptives	from a RELATIONSHIPS topic
Pre-reading skills	from a LANGUAGE topic

Jane started to ask questions about these part-topics. She found many that would be good to investigate.

How are toys designed commercially? What sort of people are employed to design toys? Do you have to have any qualifications relating to knowledge about children to get such employment? Do children actually need toys if they are quite happy to play with things not designed as toys; eg, old boxes, cotton reels, etc. Why do some young people have unwanted pregnancies when contraception is easily available? Are young people frightened to seek contraceptive advice? Do parents know the importance of pre-reading skills? What they are and how do you help children to acquire them?

5 Other subjects – interesting topics

You can even get an idea by thinking about topics you have enjoyed learning about in other subjects.

Examples

Mary found the work she did on prison reform in history made her think about children who are born in prison hospitals; about what it felt like as a child to visit family members in prison and how families cope when one parent is sent to prison.

Jim was fascinated by a science topic on atomic energy. He wondered about pollution, about the danger to children from nuclear waste storage arrangements. He also thought about whether children themselves feel frightened by the dangers of atomic power.

Try doing this yourself. Write all the topics you have most enjoyed in your other subjects at school/college. Think about them with young children in mind. Can you develop any investigative ideas?

6 Collecting cuttings about child-related issues

You could set this up as a class resource. Just collect any article, photograph or advertisement that has child connections. You can find them in magazines, newspapers or pamphlets. Build up a collection either in a scrap-book or stored loose in an envelope file. Looking through such a collection will often spark off an idea for further study.

Have you ever thought what it must be like to be at the centre of a big press story? Just imagine what it is like for a child in that situation. What would it be like to be in the public eye all the time? Imagine what it is like for a royal child. Would it affect their development? How could you find out?

Pedal power for royal cyclists

The Prince and Princess of Wales and their two sons, Prince Henry and Prince William (right), taking to the road on Tresco mid-way through a holiday on the Isles of Scilly to coincide with the boys' half-term break. The Prince will attend a ceremony on the neighbouring island of St Mary's tomorrow, when the isles' cable will be linked to the national grid.

7 Listening to other students' ideas for an investigation

No, you should not just copy someone else's idea. You will never do as well on an idea that is not your own. There are strict rules about it anyway. But finding out what others are doing is a good way of triggering an idea for you.

Example

You listen to someone explaining that they have decided to investigate how much pocket money parents feel their children should be given.

You could decide to look at the other side of the same idea by asking children what they want pocket money for. Do they save to buy something they want or is it all spent on sweets and chocolates? By changing the idea you have made it your own.

If you have worked through some of these suggestions for getting an idea you may find that you have got several and do not know how to choose the best one to develop. That is a good position to be in, providing you do not waste much time in making up your mind. If this is your problem, one way of helping you to decide is to clarify *how* you would go about investigating each of your ideas. You can then choose to go ahead with the one that will be the most straightforward in terms of the time it would take and the resources available to you. Remember that people are a resource.

Example

Back to our friend John. He chose to analyse what children could learn by walking through the park with an adult. He did this because he could do much of it by observation. He knew that he took two small children to the park every Sunday afternoon. He had ample opportunity to note the plants, animals, insects, people, colours, shapes in the park surroundings and he could talk about them to his brothers' children. As part of his investigation he made a set of matching cards with two each of variously shaped leaves on them. The children learned the names of the trees and bushes the leaves came from by playing Snap and Memory games with them. This practice helped them to take an interest in the plants growing in the park.

PART
2

Technological Assignments

Questioning the effects of technology

1 What is technology?

Technology is a word frequently used in today's society. Even so it is difficult to define. What does it mean to you?

Write a brief definition of what you think it means; share your thoughts with one or two other students in your class.

Don't worry if all your ideas vary. It has taken the so-called experts a long while to start agreeing on what they mean by the word.

It is important that you understand what is meant by a technological activity because this section of the book has some for you to do.

Read the following definition:

'Technology is the means of modifying the environment to meet human needs.'

With a partner, **list** some ways in which the environment has been modified to meet human needs. Try to think of an example from the home, the provision of health, coping with extremes of climate and the needs of children.

Spend some time discussing with the rest of the class the examples you have generated. You might also like to think about the following issues:

- Who decides what human needs are?
- Is technology always a good thing?

If you look back to the definitions you came up with at the beginning of this assignment you will probably find that there is some confusion about the word. This is because the word 'technology' can mean both an activity and a modern piece of equipment. Some people call the results of a technological activity 'technology'.

For example, think of a computer. This is an artefact (a thing made by people). It was produced as a result of a technological activity. It was designed to satisfy the human need to change the environment by making a device that would store and process information that could be retrieved very quickly – quicker than the human brain.

So what is a technological activity? It is an activity that is always:
- Creative
- Practical
- Problem-solving
- Concerned with human needs
- Is aimed at producing an artefact, environment or a system which will affect people and/or control some aspect of the way they live.
- One that uses knowledge and skills from many different subject areas.
- *It is usually a co-operative endeavour that produces something new — an innovation.*

With a partner, spend a few minutes **deciding why** it is usually best done as a co-operative endeavour?

With the same partner decide whether the following descriptions are of technological activities.

Mandy's Party

When Mandy was seventeen, she had her right leg amputated after doctors had diagnosed a bone tumour at the lower end of the femur. This meant that she spent many months in hospital after the operation. She underwent a course of chemotherapy which resulted in her hair falling out and she needed much medical and psychological support to learn to live with her artificial limb. Before she was ill she had been a very lively, athletic girl. She was still in hospital as her eighteenth birthday approached. Her friends decided to plan a party for her and asked her parents if they, too, wanted to be part of the group who planned it. The friends and her parents wanted the party to try and give Mandy a lift, as she had been rather depressed with her circumstances and the effects of chemotherapy which she had not quite completed. They decided to provide a tea party for the whole ward. They talked to the doctor and nurses about what foods would be best for Mandy and the other patients, and asked their permission to set up the table and music in the ward on the day of the party. They sent invitations to all the patients and arranged for Mandy's favourite pop star to make a surprise visit. They shared out the tasks involved in having the meal ready, the music chosen and taped, and organising how the things they needed would get taken to the hospital. One of the group arranged to meet the pop star at the hospital entrance and make sure he found Mandy's ward. A long discussion between all the friends and Mandy's parents took place about what the birthday cake should be. The medical advice had been that none of the patients could eat a lot; what they needed was food that would encourage them to eat a little. They came up with lots of ideas and finally decided that a 'cake' made out of sorbet ice-cream would be the best solution. They had to plan how to keep it from melting until it was time to cut the cake and how to make it into a birthday cake especially for Mandy. They solved this problem by experimenting with piping an icing sugar greeting on to a block of sorbet and finding out whether candle-holders would stay in sorbet once it got a bit soft. These solutions worked and they planned to make the cake from a fancy sorbet made for twenty people. Mandy enjoyed her party, although she and her fellow patients got tired quicker than the group had planned. It did make her perk up and once her course of chemotherapy had finished she recovered quickly.

Recording Pupil Records

Ms Smith, the headteacher of a comprehensive school, decided to computerise all the records of her pupils. Before she decided to do this record cards were filed by each Head of Year, and recorded pupil achievements in the way of examination results, certification for swimming, sports and first-aid, attendance records and decisions made about pupils' needs. In the same school the school nurse kept record cards with details of individual pupil's medical history, immunisation records and results of hearing tests and routine school medical examinations. Ms Smith bought a commercially designed computer program that allowed all details of each pupil to be entered in a computer file for that particular pupil. She arranged to be registered as a *Data User* under the UK Data Protection Act 1984, getting the necessary registration forms from a main post office near the school. She wrote a letter to parents explaining that, whereas only the nurse and the school doctor could access the medical part of the data, teachers would be able to use the system and add to it. She talked to the teaching staff about her intentions and set up a working party of some teachers to plan the co-ordination of the new system, the destruction of old records once they had been put on computer file, and to arrange training for staff to be able to use the new system efficiently.

Look at the diagram below:

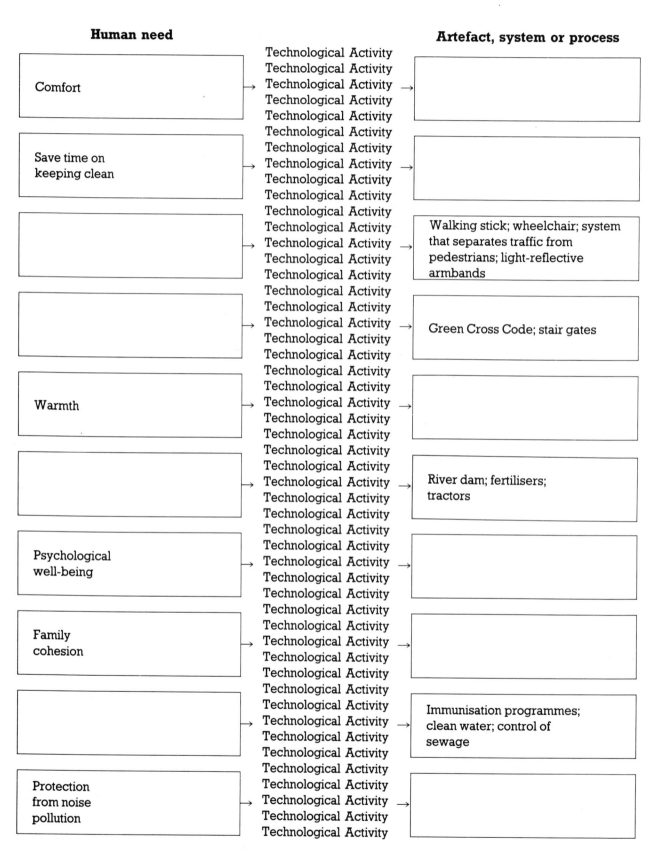

Human need

- Comfort
- Save time on keeping clean
- [blank]
- [blank]
- Warmth
- [blank]
- Psychological well-being
- Family cohesion
- [blank]
- Protection from noise pollution

Technological Activity (repeated)

Artefact, system or process

- [blank]
- [blank]
- Walking stick; wheelchair; system that separates traffic from pedestrians; light-reflective armbands
- Green Cross Code; stair gates
- [blank]
- River dam; fertilisers; tractors
- [blank]
- [blank]
- Immunisation programmes; clean water; control of sewage
- [blank]

In a small group try and **fill in the empty boxes** on the diagram. If you don't have a photocopy, draw a rough copy on a large sheet of paper.

You are probably already users of many devices and systems that have been produced as a result of technological activity. Inventing new and easier ways of doing things has been part of history. Think about the planning, experimenting and evaluating that produced the motor car or the modern house. We can often use the new devices and systems to help us with technological activities. So many of the modern devices are now used in industry, commerce and in the home. All young people need to be skilled in keyboard use, computerised transactions and computer-aided manufacturing.

Study the following flow-chart that illustrates the technological process:

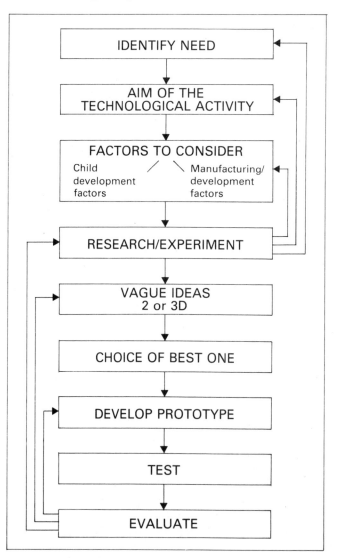

Some of the processes and products that have resulted from technological developments have served minor needs of people at the expense of rather more major ones. We as people have an urgent need to attend to the changing weather patterns that have been caused by a build-up of carbon dioxide and other gases in the layers around our atmosphere. We are in danger of losing parts of the land we live on. Some land will be flooded by the rising sea-level as the ice caps melt in the warmer weather conditions. We know the major causes of this build-up of gases. It has been caused by the burning of fossil fuels, the destruction of large areas of the earth's rain forests and the production of methane from the increased quantities of organic waste.

If we are to control these environmental changes, people across the world need to work together to produce solutions.

In small groups, **list** as many reasons as you can for why that might be difficult. Share your ideas with the rest of the class.

As a class, decide why the resolution of such a major environmental problem is important for the future generations of children. The following quote from a TV chat show might help.

> 'We do not inherit the earth. We just borrow it for our kids.'
>
> *Ben Elton, 26 April 1989*

If you would like to, do one of the following:
1 Design a poster that helps people understand what technology is.
2 List some human needs that have not, as yet, been met.
3 Write an article trying to persuade readers that the car is a selfish style of transportation.
4 Collect tips from people about how ordinary people can save energy at home, at school/college and in the workplace. If you did this as a group you could go on and produce a booklet to sell for a charity.

2 Does technology affect childhood?

Medical technology

These children were 'test-tube' babies. The girl is Louise Brown who was the first child conceived this way.

There used to be only one way to get pregnant. That is not true any more since medical researchers directed their energies to the human problem of infertility. Couples who wanted children but who did not manage to achieve them in the normal way had little help available. Adoption of other people's children was their only way of starting a family. As less and less children became available for adoption, many couples remained childless. Since the mid-1970s, the complex solutions of artificial insemination and *in vitro* fertilisation improve the chances of couples achieving their desire to have a family.

Both sperm and embryos can be stored over a period of many years, prior to use for successful insemination and implantation.

This particular technological technique brings with it many problems which have yet to be resolved. Mostly, the problems are moral, ethical and legal.

For example, Mr and Mrs C. from Nevada, USA, went through the process of defying infertility. Using the new scientific techniques now available, four embryos were developed outside the human body. Just before the implantation stage, when doctors would have put the embryos into the uterus of Mrs C., hoping that at least one of them would embed into the lining of her uterus (womb) ready to develop normally, both Mr and Mrs C. were killed in a car crash. The embryos remain in storage ten years later whilst the law courts try and decide what should happen to them.

What do you think?

Discuss what should happen to the embryos. Who should make the decisions about them?

Various opinions have been suggested. These are some of them:
- The embryos should be implanted into other women wanting a child.
- The embryos should be used by medical workers researching the effects of the storage system on human embryos.
- The embryos should be destroyed.

With a partner, **decide** what you think should happen to the four embryos. In a small group, discuss the possibility of preventing such dilemmas. Propose a solution if you can.

Share your suggestions with the rest of the class.

How many parents and doctors, throughout time, must have wished they could see the unborn child? To do so would mean that fears could be allayed, abnormalities excluded. Nowadays we have this facility. Ultrasound scanning devices allow the developing baby to be checked for normal development, to check how many babies are developing and to make sure that they are growing as they should. It is also possible to take small samples of cells from the placenta or the fluid around the foetus. Examination of these cells in a laboratory identifies the sex of the unborn child and determines whether the child will be born with a hereditary disease. These tests are called chorion-villus sampling (CVS) and amniocentesis. Both these cell-sampling tests carry a risk of miscarriage, amniocentesis being more hazardous than CVS.

It is even possible, now, for surgery to be performed on the unborn child. Thus some problems could be put right even before birth. Micro-surgical techniques make this possible although it is still a very rare and difficult procedure.

In small groups, **decide** what you think about these 'modifications to the environment'. Is it always a good idea to know that your unborn child is to be handicapped? Does it matter whether you know the sex of your baby before it is born? Should a child's life be put at risk by a cell-sampling test before birth?

Share your thoughts with the rest of the class.

The following graph shows the decline in infant mortality over a considerable period of time.

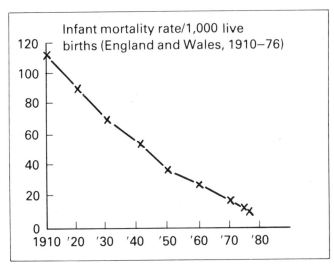

Infant mortality rate/1,000 live births (England and Wales, 1910–76)

In groups, discuss this graph and suggest reasons why so many children used to die so young. **Consider** why the numbers have dropped so dramatically. As a whole class, share your suggestions and make a list of them on the blackboard.

Do you know which of your suggestions had the *greatest* effect in helping children to stay alive?

Some further work on this topic could be:
1   List any anxieties you have as a result of thinking about technology and children's health.

2   Compose a speech that would persuade a National Health Service committee to allocate more money to the health of children.
3   Draw a flow-chart showing the antenatal care of women in the UK. You will need to do some research to do this accurately. You could talk to a woman who has had a recent pregnancy.
4   Discuss with a partner what might be the religious objections to *in vitro* fertilisation.

3 Does technology affect the everyday life of children?

Shopping

Read the following scenario:

A young child is taken shopping with her parents. They take her to a large hypermarket. A big trolley is pushed around this vast store and the parents fill it with a variety of goods ready to take to the checkout point. In this store, which has a catalogue, prices are not displayed, only bar codes are attached to each item. At the checkout, the goods are paid for by one parent writing a cheque or offering a credit card.

Discuss these points:
• What do you think this child thinks shopping is about?
• Will she learn anything about money values or money calculation?
• Will she understand anything other than that her parents could pick out what they wanted and take it home with them?

Read the following scenario about a different shopping outing with the same child:

It is 10.30 am, the mother and child walk up the road to the local shops. The mother goes in to a small corner shop to buy milk, bread and a jar of coffee. On producing her purse to pay for the goods, she finds she has only 20p in it. 'I will be back in a moment,' she explains to the shopkeeper. She goes to the local cashpoint, gets out a card and after inserting it into the machine and pressing a few buttons comes away holding a handful of banknotes. They go back to the shop, where the mother pays for the goods she wanted. They go home.

Discuss the following:
- Where do you think this child believes money comes from?
- Do you think she believes it is given away to anyone who wants it?

Read what happens to her on another shopping trip, this time to buy the weekly groceries:

Her mother has a list, father is pushing the trolley, the child is pottering along behind. As the parents choose the food items they wish to purchase, the child spots various delights set out on display at her eye-level. Each time she sees something she would like – Smarties, little packets of cereal, cake decorations in tiny jars, she puts them in the trolley along with the rest of the shopping. Father notices and says, 'No, we don't need that.' The child protests and the parents get cross. She cannot understand why she, too, cannot have what she wants.

Decide the following:
- Do you think the shops set out the items attractive to children at their eye-level on purpose?
- Is the child's behaviour logical?
- How can a child learn that money is not in endless supply and has to be used carefully?

Ask some people over 50 years or so what happened before these technological systems and devices made money transactions so quick. Do you think the time is coming, as in parts of the USA, where shops will not deal in notes and coins – only in 'paper money'? Will that make it even more difficult for children to learn about money?

Preparing food

Make a list of what you've eaten in the last 24 hours. Tick those food items on your list that were prepared from the raw ingredients.

It is possible these days, to eat nothing other than foods already prepared and cooked. All the purchaser has to do is to heat them up if they are to be eaten hot. Very few children experience helping a parent to prepare and bake bread, pies, cakes and biscuits. It is possible for children never to see a salad being washed and prepared for eating.

More and more pre-prepared vegetables, meat and baked products are sold almost ready for the table. This is the result of food scientists developing the technology of food preservation, hygienic packaging, additives that help retain colour, shape and texture of foods, food storage and transportation.

Thus a child might well not understand much about where foods originate or how they are made ready and safe for eating. You might like to read an investigation that a pupil did at the time of a baby-food scare in 1989 on page 118.

Family activities

Study the graph below:

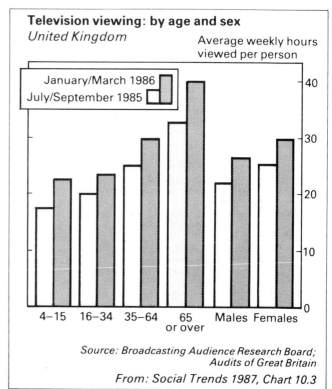

Television viewing: by age and sex
United Kingdom   Average weekly hours viewed per person

January/March 1986
July/September 1985

Source: Broadcasting Audience Research Board; Audits of Great Britain
From: Social Trends 1987, Chart 10.3

As a group, decide how much TV, on average, you watch each week.

Discuss what you remember from your own childhood about TV watching; playing family games such as Ludo and Monopoly, and visits to friends or entertaining other families.

Decide whether the technological developments that have brought us TV, home computers, computer games and toys, cassette players with earphones, radio and music systems have affected the development of young children?

Share your ideas with the rest of the class, prior to choosing to do one of the following as either a group, a pair or an individual:

1   Plan an activity for nursery aged children (3–5 years) that would help them to understand how the basic ingredients of one or two ready-made dishes are grown, what they look like before processing and what needs to be done to them to prepare them for cooking.

2   Write a short pamphlet promoting the idea of children watching less TV. The pamphlet is for parents, to help them understand the effects on young children of spending time watching TV at the expense of other experiences with their families.

3   Plan a topic on 'Money' that could be part of the infant school curriculum. Decide what experiences, visits and activities could be part of this topic work to help the children understand the various money transactions they see.

4   Investigate technological changes to the play experiences at home or in the nursery. You could do this by visiting a toy museum and a toy shop to find out the types of materials used in toy manufacture over a period of time.

4 Does technology affect children's learning at school?

Look carefully at the photos and note the differences between the two. Pay particular attention to any clues in the photographs that help you to discover any differences in the ways that primary children are being helped to learn.

Research has found that children learn best by doing; not by copying what the teacher has done, but by being actively involved in the job they are asked to do. Before this was understood children learned much by rote, learning to read in a very mechanical way, learning to calculate by doing sums. They were often in a position where they could read a book but not understand it and do their sums, even quite complicated ones, without understanding what they had done or how to apply those calculations to real situations. So children could add, subtract, multiply and divide money sums but not be able to work out the change a shopkeeper gave when they went on errands for their parents.

Nowadays, schools concentrate on trying to help children understand, to enjoy reading a good story, having an interesting conversation, working out the solution to a real problem and generally making sense of the world as they experience it.

Technological developments have provided children with many more of the tools they need to be able to learn in a way that brings understanding and motivates them to be curious to learn more. The materials that children use are more varied and are often made of safe, unbreakable plastic. Books are still used, but videos, audio-tapes and slides, film and computer information bases are now added to the sources of information available to learn from. Children still write on their pictures and on paper in exercise books, but they also write using a computer to word-process their ideas. Hand-held calculators are used to solve mathematical problems and work out their own technological solutions to problems that help them to understand scientific principles.

There are, of course, constraints on this approach to early learning. As a group, **brainstorm** what might be the difficulties. Think of the difficulties for the provider, probably the Local Education Authority; the teacher; the parents and the children. **Share** your thoughts with the whole class and **discuss** the possible solutions to some of these difficulties.

If you have time, you could do one of the following:

1   Suggest ways in which parents could be helped to understand modern teaching methods in the primary schools.

2   Role-play a conversation between a local councillor who wants to spend more money on resources for primary education and one who believes that young children do not need such sophisticated and varied learning materials.

3   Talk to some older people about their primary education. Find out what they think about the education provided for children these days. Write a short report to share what you discover with the rest of the class. If you prefer, you could tape your discussion and the tape could be used in the future as a class resource.

4   If you can find one, compare a reading book of 20–30 years ago with one being used in a local primary school now. Make a list of the differences. Which one do you think is best for the purposes of learning to read? Note your reasons.

The Technological Process

1 Analysing problems to be solved

Read the following newspaper extract:

Drive to help mothers at work in 1990s

By Robin Oakley and Roland Rudd

The Government is preparing plans to mount a big publicity drive, similar to its single European market campaign, to force employers to provide child care facilities for working mothers.

The move comes after startling new figures have shown that four in five new jobs will have to be taken by women in less than 10 years.

Consider the following issues:
- Why can't women use their existing local child-care facilities?
- Should mothers work and let other people look after their children?
- Should fathers work and let other people look after their children?
- How could the employers justify the expense of providing a workplace crèche?
- What would parents want from a crèche facility at work?
- Should it be available for men and women on the workforce payroll?

- What might be the advantages and disadvantages to the employer, the parents and the children?
- How do employers know enough about the needs of young children to be able to provide such a facility? Would they need to contract the work to people who do?

Each group should take one of the issues and decide what they already know and think about the issue. They should then decide what they still need to know to be able to give a fair answer to the question. **Record** your ideas and the investigations you would need to do to produce an answer. If you did this recording on to large sheets of paper, they could be displayed for everyone to see and discuss together.

If you want to try further analytical work on this problem, do one of the following:

1 Make a list of the advantages and disadvantages of both parents working full-time. What are the implications for the family income and expenditure, family activities and children's feelings.

2 Role-play a discussion between a woman who has decided she would like to return to work, placing her 3-year-old child in a workplace crèche, and her husband who is not so keen on the idea.

3 Imagine you are a working parent with a small child attending the workplace crèche. You have been elected on to its management committee and you are campaigning for longer opening hours for the crèche. At present it opens 15 minutes before work starts and closes 10 minutes after work finishes. Write your campaign

speech giving reasons why you would prefer it to stay open longer on some days of the week.

4   Make a list of the ways a family could save money in order to make it possible for one parent to stay at home with the pre-school children.

2 Getting vague ideas recorded

Read the following newspaper article before brainstorming as a class all your ideas for ways of providing childcare for working parents.

Inside a pre-school profit centre

AS I walked into the showplace Kinder-Care nursery in Granada Hills, a comfortable Los Angeles suburb, satisfied district manager Sam Mazzulo was ready to prove how providing child care and running a profitable business can be one and the same thing.

'You can choose to sell cigarettes or any other kind of product. In our case, the product is the care the children receive,' explained Sam, a savvy Californian businessman who used to own and manage supermarkets.

At Granada Hills there are many reminders that this is no ordinary nursery but part of a highly organised, rigidly standardised, big business group.

'We open at 6.30 in the morning and close at six at night, and serve the children with breakfast, lunch, morning and afternoon snacks from a standard menu varied for local tastes,' says nursery director Merrily Mellin.

'The majority are here for the full working day — 8.15 till 5.30. We provide learning and socialising opportunities that they don't get at home.

'What big business can do is provide comprehensive training,' says Sam Mazzulo proudly. 'For instance, we guarantee parents that our infant helpers have all seen a film on how to change nappies by the most sanitary means possible.'

Kinder-Care mothers get blow-by-blow reports of their children's progress, even if they are not old enough to crawl. The 'Infant Daily Activity Report' in the babycare room lists every one of junior's achievements, right down to a bowel movement.

Enthusiasm

Kinder-Care considers all its children educable from the age of two — and that means more than just music, finger-painting and dressing up. 'There's a push to introduce science in here, so we've put in some goldfish,' Merrily points out with enthusiasm in the twos' room.

Half the threes are working on a wildlife book and the other half are outside in a well-equipped playground that would be the envy of many a British nursery.

Kinder-Care finds a second source of profit in before and after-school care. Children aged six to 12 can be dropped off by parents to be bussed to school, picked up in the afternoon and taken care of for the remainder of their parents' working day. Business is booming to the extent that in some states Kinder-Cares operate night and day shifts. Company profits are $21 million a year and growing.

But I left with an uneasy feeling that Kinder-Care and its clones were taking on more than the safe custody and stimulation of children in their charge: what is on offer is surrogate parenthood from Monday to Friday at an all-in cost of 93 dollars a week.

What really made me sad was Merrily Mellin's account of why Kinder-Care, which closes only on major holidays, like Christmas, gets particularly busy on bank holidays even though parents are home themselves. 'The fact is, these parents don't want to bake and ice cookies with their kids or get playdough all over their nice carpets,' explains Merrily. 'We do ALL that messy stuff here, and that's part of why they send them.'

FUN TIME: In a Kinder-Care playground

When you have noted all the ideas your class can suggest, work in small groups to **make notes, sketches, plans** of any of the ideas that you think might work. Each group should develop, in rough, at least three different ideas. It's best if all the group members work on one idea at a time.

Whilst you are doing this, points will crop up that you will need to find out about. Make a note of these queries as you go along. You might also be able to suggest ways those points could be clarified.

It will take time for each group to **present** their ideas, but unless you do that you will not be able to find the best idea to work on. The sharing of ideas is an important part of the technological process. Others listening or looking at your ideas might see advantages or disadvantages to your solution that you had not realised.

If you'd like further practice at getting vague ideas together ready for sharing and discussing their possibilities, choose one of the following to do:

1   Your teacher has been allocated an extra £50 to spend on providing resources for the course you are studying. Record all your vague ideas about how best it could be spent – you will need reasons.

2   Imagine you work for an employer who has decided to provide a workplace crèche. Your boss has asked you to come up with some ideas about the play materials and equipment that should be provided. Make a list of all the points you would need to know about the crèche before you could carry out this task. Having thought of the questions, give yourself hypothetical answers so that you can come up with your vague ideas about the provision of play materials and equipment.

3   The workplace crèche your child attends has found that they have a safety problem. The entrance to the crèche needs to be locked to prevent the children wandering off, yet the staff wish to encourage parents to come and see their children during their tea-breaks and lunch hours. They need a system that would allow both to happen. There are 50 parents with children attending the crèche. Record as many ideas as you can for solving the problem.

4   Some parents who leave their children at a crèche have particular dietary requirements for their children. What systems can you think off to make sure that children are only offered food their parents would like them to eat? Record as many ideas as you can.

3 Choosing the best idea

Look at the following vague ideas generated about the problem of providing childcare facilities for working parents. You may well have other ideas that your class generated in the previous assignment. Use all the ideas, yours and the ones below.

WORKPLACE CRÈCHE

A   Firm buys in a pre-packaged crèche. Sets it up and charges partial costs to parents of either sex wishing to use it for their children.

B   Firm sets up its own crèche, using own facilities. Pays for all costs. Gets trained workers to care for children. Parents from workforce elected to serve on a monitoring committee to make sure children's needs are catered for. Committee meetings held in working hours.

C   Same as B. Committee meetings held outside working hours.

D   Firm organises a scheme whereby a woman can choose to build up hours of work to suit age/needs of child. Firm agree to employ her as and when she can cope with her child spending a longer time in the crèche. Therefore, a woman could start off working 2 hours a week when the child is 1 year old and build up to 6 hours a day, when child aged $4\frac{1}{2}$ years.

ALTERNATIVES

1   Tax-relief on money spent by working women on the necessary childcare arragements.

2   Extra child benefit paid by Government to parents who are both working.

Both **1 + 2** would enable private arrangements to be made.

3   Firm supports local education pre-school provision, paying for improved facilities and extra sessions before and after school; eg, 8.30 am – 6.00 pm.

4   Firm encourages husband and wife employment – so between them they can work an extra-long day. The childcare can be shared between them. Tea provided by workplace for families at swapover time; eg, father works 7.30 am – 4.30 pm. Mother brings child/children to workplace for tea. Father takes child/children home. Mother works from 4.30 pm – 9.00 pm. Costs to firm very inexpensive compared to crèche.

5   Firm employs a childminder co-ordinator. Her job is to facilitate co-operative groups of women; eg, 3 mothers share 2 jobs plus childcare of all children involved. Could be on 2 weeks work, 1 week childcare. Firm pays for 3 jobs. Mothers to negotiate how often they swap roles.

How can you decide which is the best idea to develop?

In groups, **decide** whether there are any ideas too expensive to pursue. Eliminate any solutions that overlook the needs of the children.

Which idea is the simplest yet would still solve the problem?

Decide whether there are any other factors, apart from
• Expense
• Needs of young children
• Simplicity
that would help you to choose between all these ideas. Perhaps you would prefer to combine two or more of them to provide the best solution?

Would you need to make any investigations to help you to decide whether an idea is feasible? Take no. 3, for example: how would the Local Education Authority view sponsorship? Does the Education Reform Act 1988 mean that individual schools could liaise with industry on such a project without the approval of the Local Education Authority?

Take time to go through the possibilities carefully. Look at the advantages and disadvantages of each idea in terms of the children, the parent/s, the other employees, the employers and the Government. One of your group should **take brief notes** to help you decide which idea is the best. Once you have made that decision, write down your reasons for choosing as you did.

If you have the time, try one of the following to help you practice choosing sensibly:

1   Use a mail order catalogue to choose a present for a child you know. You will have to have vague ideas of what the child needs; what her/his age and interests are; what price you would be prepared to pay, and what would be good value for money.
2   Choose the foods you would need to make a healthy mid-day meal for yourself and a friend. You have only £1.50 to spend. Write down what you would buy and why you chose these foods. Explain why you consider the meal to be a healthy one.

3   A friend of yours is ill and has asked you to take him a newspaper to read in hospital. Look at a cross-section of daily newspapers and decide which one to buy him. Your local library will usually have a selection of newspapers for you to look at. You will have to think about what your friend's interests and reading ability are before you decide. Jot down the reasons for your choice.
4   Look in the local paper at the job vacancies. Choose one that would suit you best. List your reasons for that choice.

4   Making a prototype

In the technological process (see p. xx) it is at this stage, after choosing the best idea, the time comes to develop the idea in detail. If it is a system or environment you are developing then you would think through your chosen idea in great detail, communicating the idea in words and diagrams. You would work out the costs involved and schedule its timing. You would also need to communicate the implications of implementing the new environment or system.

However, if the brief you are working on requires an artefact to solve the problem, then at this stage you should make a prototype.

A prototype is the first product made as a single item which is tested so that its design can be changed, if necessary, before mass-production begins. This is an important stage of the technological process. This is where design faults can be identified and the design modified. Ideas that seemed good in theory sometimes do not work in practice. They may be too difficult to achieve, too expensive or too complex for the purpose. Evaluating as you work through the technological process helps to produce the best solution to the problem.

Let us suppose that you have already analysed a problem about the difficulties in teaching young children the mathematical rules of addition, subtraction, multiplication and division. You have come up with the solution of creating a game that would make the learning enjoyable for infant-aged schoolchildren. You have already thought of some vague ideas and have decided what was your best idea. This is shown overleaf.

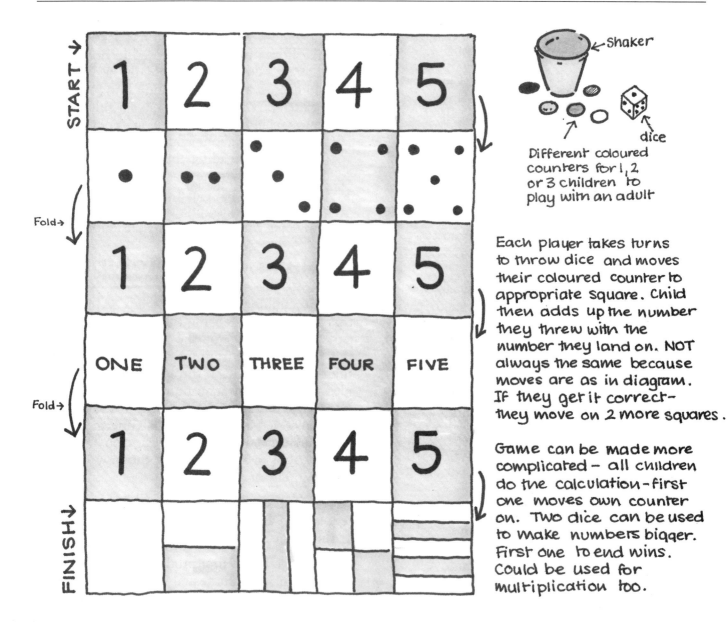

Different coloured counters for 1, 2 or 3 children to play with an adult

Each player takes turns to throw dice and moves their coloured counter to appropriate square. Child then adds up the number they threw with the number they land on. NOT always the same because moves are as in diagram. If they get it correct — they move on 2 more squares.

Game can be made more complicated — all children do the calculation — first one moves own counter on. Two dice can be used to make numbers bigger. First one to end wins. Could be used for multiplication too.

In groups, **decide** exactly how you are going to make your prototype. You will need to decide on size, method of construction, materials needed, how to make it so it will stay looking attractive; what type of lettering, what case, what type of numbers, eg. 4 or 4, how will the game be stored and packaged; do you need to have written rules?

Make your prototype as a group sharing the tasks between you. Note the costs of the materials you use. Make clear notes justifying all the decisions you make as you go along.

If you have time, you could:
1 Play the game yourselves to see how well it works. Note any problems with the design that need changes.
2 List the games, songs, stories and rhymes that helped you to learn to count, add, subtract, multiply and divide.
3 Work out exactly how much your prototype cost to make:
Allow £10 per hour for the use of your school premises (heating/lighting, etc.)
Allow £15 per hour for the cost of the supervisor's salary (your teacher)
Allow £5 per hour for the workers' salaries (your group)
Add the cost of the materials you used.
Write down why making a prototype is more expensive than mass-production.
How does the making of a prototype save money in industry?
4 Make a travel version of the same game. This could be used to keep a child occupied whilst flying to a sunny holiday.

5 Testing your prototype

You will not know if your game is actually suitable for 5–7-year-olds unless you test it with children of this age.

You will also need to know how well your construction of it stands up to use by children.

In your groups, **plan** your testing procedures. Remember that testing should be fair. You will need to plan
- How you are going to get access to children of the right age.
- How many different children you need to try it with to get a fair idea of the game's usefulness in terms of its purpose.
- What you are going to look for as children play the game.
- How you are going to find out if it is too easy or too difficult for children of this age.
- How you are going to record what you observe as well as play the game with the children. Remember the game needs an adult who can add up accurately to play it properly.
- What tests you are going to design to find out
  (a) how durable the game pieces are;
  (b) how dirty and unattractive it becomes with use;
  (c) how safe it is.

Once you have a group plan for testing your game, **negotiate** its feasibility with your teacher. If necessary, alter your plan to make it feasible. Don't take such a long time arranging for your testing procedure to be carried out that you lose interest. It is best done as soon as possible.

Once you have tested your product you should analyse carefully what you have found out.

If you want more practice thinking about testing procedures, do one of the following:
1 Look at a copy of *Which*, the consumer magazine that carries out testing of a variety of consumer goods. Choose a product that interests you and read about how it was tested and what the results were.
2 Design a testing procedure for potato crisps. You could use it every time you buy a different make of crisps to see how the different products compare. You'll need to think of a fair test. You'll need to think about what you expect from a good packet of crisps.
3 Design a poster expressing a message you feel strongly about; eg, 'Don't smoke near me'.
   or
   Design a new logo for an organisation you approve of.

Test out whether the poster or logo has achieved its purpose. You might need to ask a variety of people what 'message' they get from studying your design. Do the test results make you think you should alter your design in some way?
4 Describe your feelings and justify future actions you might take as a result of finding out that the toiletries you use are tested on animals in the prototype stage of manufacture.

6 Evaluating the technological process

If you have worked through the previous five assignments in this book you have nearly completed a practice of the technological process. You have analysed a problem to be solved; generated vague ideas that might solve the problem; chosen your best idea; and made and tested a prototype.

The last stage is one of the most important. You now have the task of **reviewing** the whole process and making firm conclusions about the end-product you have achieved.

To evaluate you need to **consider**:
- Was each stage of the process given enough time, thought and energy?
- Were important points overlooked or wrongly emphasised?
- What were the constraints on a successful outcome?
- What positive factors helped the process?
- Were any investigations that were carried out fair and to the point?
- Does the end-product need any adjustments in the light of the test results?

- Has the whole process been effectively communicated through words, diagrams and graphics where necessary?

In groups, **read** the following description of some students' work on the first three stages of the brief to help children learn one or two mathematical rules by producing a game for infant-school-aged children. As you read what they did you should be beginning to evaluate it, noting comments as you go along.

Analysis of the problem to be solved

The students decided that:
- All children need to learn the four mathematical rules of addition, subtraction, multiplication and division.
- They are usually learned at school.
- Before they can learn them, they need to be able to recognise and identify the symbols for numbers.
- They need to enjoy learning otherwise they'll get put off.
- Games and activities are more fun than doing sums.
- The game would need to suit their developmental stage; ie, it should be simple and have straightforward rules that make it fair.
- They might need to play any game with an adult who could monitor the rules.
- It would need to be challenging without being so difficult that they were put off.
- The game would need to be attractive to children – colourful and clear.
- If there were too many game pieces they would get lost.
- Children are quite rough in handling items, so any game would need to be strongly made.
- The way it was stored should be one that children can do themselves – this encourages them to be independent.

Queries they had: possible need for investigations

- Which of the four mathematical rules do they learn first or do they learn them all at once?
- How much number knowledge do they have already?
- What games are already available for this purpose and are they effective?

The group decided to ask a primary schoolteacher to visit them and discuss the points they were unsure about. They also asked this teacher to bring with her some games she used to help children. The schoolteacher explained that she could not leave her school to visit the students, but she invited them to visit her classroom after her small pupils had gone home. From this visit the students learned that:

(a) most children at five could count to ten if you asked them to;
(b) however, if you asked them to count out ten buttons or counters from a pile most of them got it wrong;
(c) they did not understand that the number you counted corresponded to the number of buttons;
(d) this proved that the numbers they counted had very little meaning for them;
(e) children needed lots of practice at counting real objects before they can learn to add and take away;
(f) multiplication and division were rules generally understood after they had learned to add and take away;
(g) the games available tended to be too complex for this age-group.

Vague ideas first thought of by this group of students

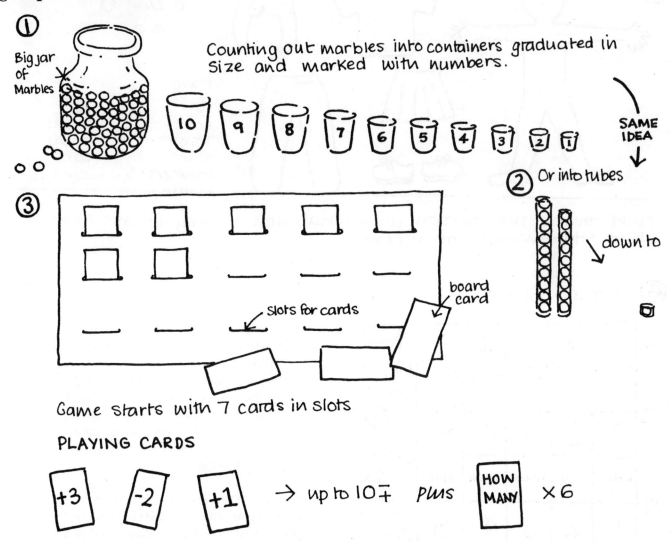

① Big jar of Marbles

Counting out marbles into containers graduated in size and marked with numbers.

SAME IDEA

② Or into tubes

down to

③

board card

Slots for cards

Game starts with 7 cards in slots

PLAYING CARDS

+3   -2   +1   → up to 10⁊   plus   HOW MANY ×6

Each child in turn picks up playing card from down-turned shuffled pile. Puts or takes away board cards as directed by playing card. When a **HOW MANY** card is picked they have to count how many on the board. Winner is person who fills the board / no slots empty. (Probably needs more slots

④ **Ten in a boat**

Boat shaped container for ten sailors to fit holes in boat.

Adult asks child to put:

"Two sailors in the boat"
"Take three sailors out of the boat"
"How many sailors are there in the boat — out of the boat."

Subtraction and addition learned.

⑤

Have:

1
nose
Tshirt
skirt
trousers
mouth

2
shoes
socks
ears
eyes

Child dresses the person with what you or they want. Ask child "How many?" at intervals.

⑥ **Board Game**

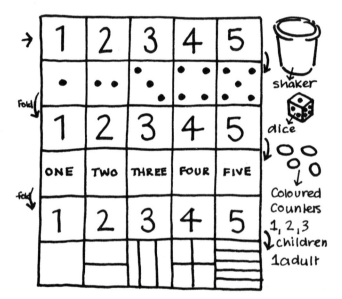

shaker

dice

Coloured Counters
1, 2, 3 children
1 adult

Each player takes turn to throw dice and moves their coloured counter to appropriate square. Child then adds up the number they threw with the number they land on. NOT always the same because moves are as in diagram. If they get it correct – move on two squares.

Game can be made more complicated – all children do the calculation – first one moves own counter on./Two dice used to make numbers bigger. First one to end wins. Could be used for multiplication too.

⑦ **Card Game called "TENS"**

Set of 60 cards

Ten look like	Ten look like	Ten look like
3	THREE	○○○

Ten look like	Ten look like	Ten look like
• • •		three

Up to 6 players given 10 cards out of shuffled pack. Each player to make up groups of cards adding up to 10. Person with most is winner.

Can be used to make up larger numbers eg 20, if fewer players.

Choosing the best one to develop further

They rejected 1 and 2 on the grounds of safety and practicality. They both had too many pieces to lose or get damaged. Children could swallow and choke on the marbles, might be tempted to take them to play with, they fitted easily into pockets etc.

They thought nos 3 and 5 had possibilities; no. 3 they thought a bit boring and would not hold a child's attention for long. It also had two sets of cards which could get muddled, torn and lost. They thought no. 5 would be quite a good idea for one child and an adult, but not so suitable for a group situation as again there were many small pieces to lose.

They had difficulty deciding between nos 6 and 7. In the end they chose no. 6 because they thought it would help a child to develop skills that could lead on to being able to play no. 7. Once children had learned to play no. 6 with an adult they could go on to play no. 7 without help.

This is where you came in!

You made the prototype and tested it.
Evaluate the whole process and **communicate** your evaluation to the rest of the class.

Display your evaluations and read carefully what other groups' criticisms were.

If you want some more practice at evaluating:
1   Evaluate the process by which a mid-day meal is made available to the pupils/students in your school/college.
2   Take any product you have recently purchased and evaluate its usefulness. Did the manufacturers make any mistakes in their design process?
3   Evaluate the activities in which you have participated to learn about the technological process. Has it helped you to understand?
4   Explain why you think a good evaluation of a product is an essential task for a commercial company.

Technological assignments 1–12

1 Brief: To devise a way to test the eyesight of a child too young to be able to respond to numbers and figures

As a whole class, **brainstorm** all the factors you will need to consider in order to do this task. Someone should write down all these factors as they are suggested.

Decide whether you know enough about the problem in order to solve it.

Suggest what investigations you will need to make at this stage. For example:
- Do you know whether babies see as clearly as an adult?
- Do you know if young children see colours as adults do?
- How is the eyesight usually tested?
- How would poor eyesight affect a child's development?
- How would colour-blindness affect a child's development?

Spend some time on your investigations before suggesting some ways that might solve the problem. When you have exhausted all your ideas, which you should record with notes and rough sketches, decide what might be the disadvantages of each idea. You may need to do further investigations before choosing one idea to define in detail.

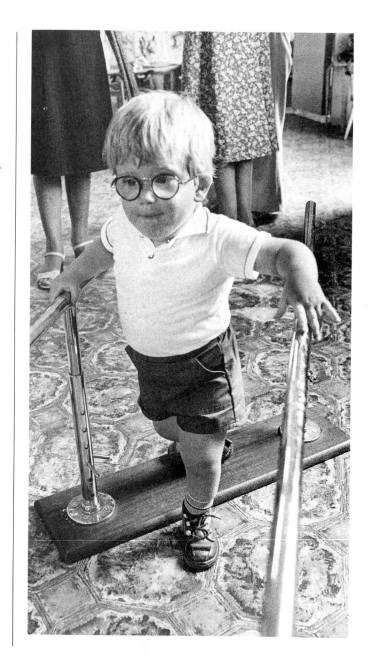

Once you have chosen a way of solving the problem, **divide** into pairs to produce a model of the product you have in mind. At this stage it is unimportant if you are constrained by the resources you have as long as you note any resources you need to bring the model up to prototype standard.

Set up a display of all the models.

Comment constructively upon each one, deciding every time you, as a class, identify a criterion that the final solution *must* fulfil. Make a list of these.

Finally, **construct** a model of the choice of final solution.

Decide how you could test its validity and reliability; that is, would it work the same way, every time it was used?

When you have achieved this, look at the flow-chart of a technological activity. How far have you worked through the process?

Decide whether it is possible for your class to complete the process. If it is possible, decide who is going to do it, where and how. Also, decide how people can share that work with the rest of the class.

If this topic area about children's eyesight has interested you, try one of the following:

1   Design a toy, book or game for a visually handicapped child of three years. The item should help the child to feel and discriminate between textures.
2   Write or tell a story designed to help a young child not to mind about wearing glasses.
3   Find out about braille. What is it? How do children learn it?
4   Talk to the mother or father of a young child with visual handicap. Find out what difficulties arise in the family because of the child's visual problem.

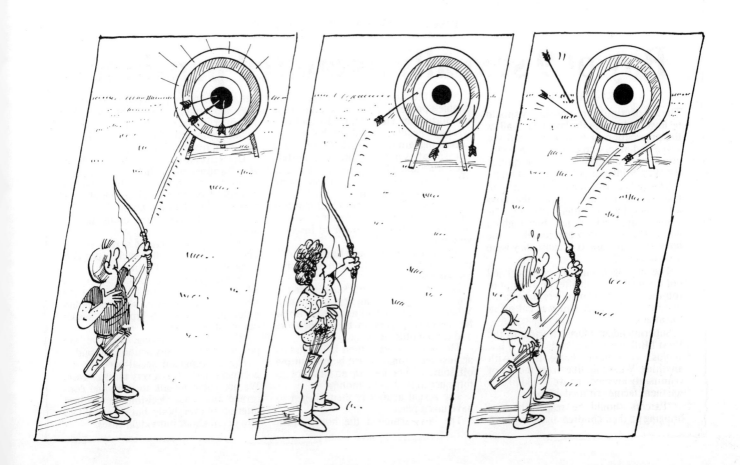

2 Brief: To develop an artefact that will encourage the young to appreciate and respect the elderly in the community

Mrs Cambell is looking after her grandchildren whilst her two married daughters have an afternoon at the shops. The grandchildren are two girls aged 2¼ years and 3½ years and three boys aged 9 months, 3¾ years and 5¼ years. Part of their time together was spent sitting in the dark of the small larder cupboard playing 'space capsules'.

Police seek lower criminality age

Boy of 9 sexually assaulted pensioner

By Craig Seton

The age of criminal responsibility should be lowered because the law did not allow the prosecution of three boys, aged six, seven and nine, who carried out a sexual attack on a disabled woman pensioner, the West Midlands police said last night.

The police said they had wanted to take criminal action against the boys after they had admitted attacking the woman, aged 63, in her Birmingham home. However, they had to deliver the boys to social workers because they were aged under 10.

The boy aged nine allegedly carried out the sexual assault after an attempt to rob the woman, who suffers from heart disease. Some of her hair was cut off in the attack.

Superintendent Martin Burton, of the West Midlands police, said: "As the law stands, we cannot charge them with anything. We would like to see the age of criminality lowered and we would like to see them facing criminal action.

"Parents should be responsible for bringing up their children, teaching them to tell the truth and respect other people's property and to look after those less fortunate. They should be told it is wrong to lie, cheat, steal and bully."

Birmingham social workers took out a place of safety order yesterday on the boy aged nine and placed him in care. The other two, who are brothers, were returned to their parents.

The police said the boys had climbed into the house of the pensioner, who is partially paralysed, through an insecure window.

The attack in the Shard End area took place on Tuesday afternoon while her husband was at work.

Detectives said the boys demanded to know where the woman kept her money. When she said she had none, they threw her personal papers on to an open fire and caused other damage.

The boy aged nine then held scissors against the woman's face before cutting off some of her hair in an attempt to force her to find some money.

The sexual assault is then alleged to have taken place.

The boys searched the house again before leaving empty handed. However, they were traced quickly by the police and interviewed with their parents. Their victim, who suffered severe shock, was receiving treatment yesterday.

Detective Inspector Tim Russell, of the Birmingham police, who investigated the case, said: "It is the worse sex offence I have seen involving children of this age. If we had not found them, they could still be out there doing this to someone else.

"It was a very serious sexual assault and I am astonished that such young lads could do such acts of depravity.

"Some people will blame videos or what they have seen on television. I am very anxious that social services should establish what lay behind the sexual nature of the assault.

"It is very worrying, but we are powerless to take any action", he said.

The Birmingham social services department said: "It is a very unusual case. We are going to talk to everyone concerned and make decisions in the best interests of everybody, but we cannot go into detail about individual cases."

The life that I want for my grandson, by Mrs Thatcher

MARGARET THATCHER wants two things for her new grandson Michael when he grows up. The strength to say No to drugs and drink abuse, and the time to talk without TV getting in the way.

The Prime Minister says she is 'absolutely thrilled' at being a grandmother and knows she may spoil the new addition to the Thatcher family. But she adds that her son Mark is extremely good with small children.

By GORDON GREIG, Political Editor

'The greatest richness you can have in life is to have been born into a family which looks after its children,' she says. 'One that doesn't smother them but brings them up to develop their own abilities.'

Mrs Thatcher, in a Woman's Own interview, looks toward the year 2000 and insists that family life and a set of accepted yardsticks are the most important things for youngsters.

'Children are the first to understand fairness,' she says. 'They expect to be told off if they're doing something they shouldn't and they understand immediately if the rule is not being applied fairly. Of course they break the rules — but they know what the rules are.'

Then, developing a theme about time and space to talk, the Prime Minister declares: 'I have a great belief that it's often easier for children to talk to grandma and grandpa than to their parents. It's vital to have this talk across the generation.

'There has been a tendency, partly due to television, to curtail a great deal of the ordinary talk and discussion between parents and children.

'It's not enough to come home to a nicely-furnished house, TV and have nice holidays if you don't give enough time to your children and do things with them. I think it's the things you do as a family that matter more than anything.'

While Mrs Thatcher believes that mothers who want to return to work should do so, she insists: 'They must make proper arrangements. I'm very much against latch key children.'

She goes on to discuss the problems of today. 'You can deal with the material things — build more hospitals, train more people.

Celebrations

'But why do some turn to violent crime? Why do some drink more than is good for them? Why do some turn to drugs? How can you stop it? And how, for the future, can you give children the strength and capacity to say No?'

The Premier admits that many marriages break up 'and in many cases it is better for the children that they do.' But it is important that standards do not deteriorate.

She says the number of children born to single-parent families is rising rapidly. 'The whole basis of our life is the family unit so we must watch these figures very carefully indeed.'

Mrs Thatcher's grandson was born in Dallas on February 28. She is expected to hold him for the first time next month when Mark and his wife Dianne join the celebrations to mark her ten years in power.

A jubilant Mrs Thatcher, with grandson Michael in her arms, in Downing Street yesterday.

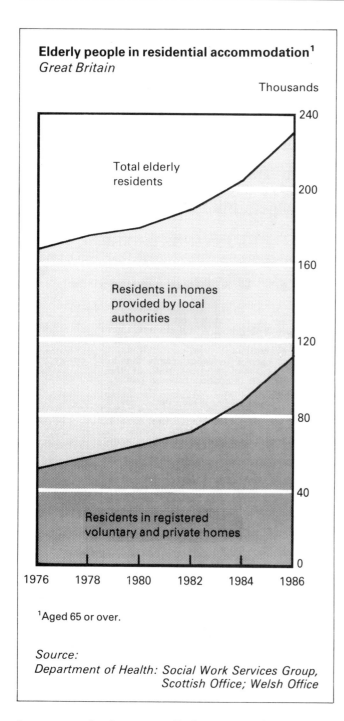

Elderly people in residential accommodation[1]
Great Britain

Thousands

Total elderly residents

Residents in homes provided by local authorities

Residents in registered voluntary and private homes

240
200
160
120
80
40
0

1976   1978   1980   1982   1984   1986

[1]Aged 65 or over.

Source:
Department of Health: Social Work Services Group,
Scottish Office; Welsh Office

In groups, **brainstorm** all the ways of encouraging the young to appreciate and respect the elderly. List *all* the ideas that are suggested.

Decide if there are any points you need to investigate.

Plan how you will do those investigations. Carry them out. Review your original ideas in the light of your investigational findings. Eliminate any ideas you now consider unsuitable.

Roughly detail those ideas you have left on your original list.

Choose the best idea to develop further. Make sure you have very clear reasons for your choice. Make sure that the chosen idea is the most useful way of solving the problem of children mistreating the elderly.

Refine your idea in great detail. Plan what materials you will need to make a prototype and how you can negotiate the use of any equipment you will need.

Make the artefact in the most efficient way you can.

Test the product you have produced. You will need to use a test that best discovers whether your idea will work.

Once you have tested your solution to the problem you should be in a position to be able to **evaluate** it.

Throughout the process, you should record what you did and why. Make notes on how the idea developed into a reality, what were the constraints on its progress and what factors helped. Decide how it could be improved. The way you worked might also need to be recorded.

Display your work for others to view and read. People inspecting the display should be given enough information to understand why your idea developed along the lines it did.

For those of you who would like to continue working on the same problem, do one of the following:
1 Propose, in writing, a new law that could help contain or eradicate the problem.
2 Make a list of the ways that the elderly could be involved with children in the community. The ways you suggest should be ones that will encourage mutual respect.
3 Why do you think that some old people are a little frightened of some adolescents in the community? Compose a song that explains why they should not be afraid.
4 Some politicians have suggested that parents should be held responsible for the misdemeanours of their children. Write or dictate a piece about what you think of that as a systems approach to the problem.

3 Brief: To develop a fair selection system

Read the following newspaper cutting. **Help** each other to understand what it is about. You will need to notice the date of the account.

14th February 2031

Official end to Parenthood for all

From his home in Central London, Joe Jackson, the Director of Europe announced the historic details of the United Kindom's population control policy. In line with all other world powers, population control measures now exist throughout the European Alliance.

Chemical additives to the water supply will provide contraceptive control in the United Kingdom. The method has been declared safe for all users of whatever age or sex. The Department of Nutrition and Health believes that the threat of imminent food rationing will now be averted. Mr Jackson, whose life interest has been to ensure a fair distribution of the world's resources, claimed last night that the result of such unified action should mean that the human race will survive.

Individuals or couples wishing to have a child must now register at a local pregnancy clinic (LPC). Those selected will be accommodated at residential centres supplied with untreated water. Details of the application and selection procedures are available at all High Street Telecommunication Points within the UK. Civil rights demonstrations were organised in most major cities yesterday. Several hundred people were arrested. An official spokesperson from the Home Office declared that such drastic changes were needed if the world as we know it is to survive. She added that population control was hardly a new idea. It had been a world issue for more than fifty years. Measures of control had been implemented as early as the 1970s and '80s in China and the sub-continent of India. Measures of control have now become considerably more sophisticated since those early beginnings as technological competence has improved.

As a group, decide what you feel about such a possibility for the future.

Write down what you think of the idea of not having the right to become a parent if you wished to.

Discuss the idea of having to select some people to be allowed to have children. Could this be done fairly? Did you know that Hitler used very cruel measures to promote one race? Any selection precedure would have to be completely fair, so as not to exclude any group of people.

Devise a way of selecting which people would have children. You could also think of ways to support those people who would have liked to have children but have been rejected by the system.

Do you know how people are selected for other situations like jobs, scholarships, prizes, Parliament? You should investigate some existing systems to see whether they could be used in this situation.

Write your ideas on a large sheet of paper so that as a class you can see what other groups have devised.

Decide which was the fairest system.

If you have time to spare you could do one of the following:

1   Write a poem that describes the feelings of a couple who cannot have the family they had hoped for.
2   Find out about China's population control policy. Write simple notes for others to read.
3   Make a list of the consequences of having fewer children in society. There may be good and bad consequences.
4   Make a list of the groups of people in our society who are unable to have children even if they want to.

4 Brief: To devise a way to encourage pregnant women to seek antenatal care

Researchers have found that women who do not seek antenatal care are more likely to have premature and complicated deliveries. They are also more likely to give birth to babies with abnormalities. The pregnant women most at risk by not seeking care during their pregnancy tend to be those who are young and/or with no fixed address.

In groups

analyse the problem to be solved;

draft several rough ideas;

decide on any investigations you might need to do;

choose your best idea;

develop that idea in detail and make a prototype if needed;

test;

evaluate.

Think about:
* Is it knowledge, skills or attitudes that need to be improved?
* Will you need to target your solutions?
* What are the reasons for one particular group of women to be most at risk? Are these reasons important to your analysis of the problem?

If you are particularly interested in this topic, try another task:

1   Role-play a schoolgirl of 16 years who has had a positive pregnancy test, talking to her best friend about her feelings.
2   Find out why people are nervous of doctors, hospitals, etc. Design a way of gathering such information.
3   Design a pamphlet for teenagers that would help them to avoid having an unwanted pregnancy.
4   Write or tape your thoughts about the father's responsibilities in relation to the care of the mother during a pregnancy. Does the father have a vested interest in the health of his unborn child?

5 Brief: To design an activity to suit Michelle, aged 7 months, immobilised by having her legs in traction

Read the following:

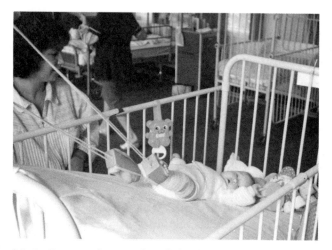

Michelle is in hospital with both legs in traction. The bed has been lowered at the head end so that the child is lying at an angle of 30° to the floor. On observation, it was noted that Michelle is often fretful. Toys have been placed around her, but often she cannot reach them. Sometimes in her efforts to reach them, the toys fall through the cot bars.

Nurses pick them up and put them back in the cot. However, she gets frustrated by not being able to touch and see her toys easily. Although she is still a baby, she enjoys being read to, especially rhymes and poems. She enjoys attention from any adult who has time to stop and talk. She tries to see what is going on around the ward but has difficulty because of the restrictive position she is in. She particularly likes toys or people who make funny noises for her. Her parents visit whenever they can, but because they have three other young children to care for, these visits cannot be extended to whole days. She goes very quiet and listless when her parents leave.

Although she can lift her head off the mattress, her neck muscles tire quite quickly. She moves her head from side to side with no problem. Her arms are free from any constraint.

Think about what activity would interest her. How can you solve the problem of her not being able to reach things and how can they be prevented from falling out of the cot through the bars?

Think about what a child of 7 months is able to do.

In groups, work through the technological process to **solve** the problem.

If you have been particularly interested in this work, attempt another task:

1 Find out about the voluntary agency that has this logo:

2 Ask the local hospital if they need any help on the children's ward. They are often very pleased to have volunteers who will read to children, play with them, mend broken toys, make doll's clothes, etc. Only do this task if you are prepared to give up some of your spare time on a regular basis.

3 Talk to the parent of a child who has been in hospital recently. Record the problems that the parents encountered as a result of this experience.

4 How can a parent prepare a child for what must be, for that child, a traumatic experience. Imagine you are a parent and have been told that your child needs an operation. The child's name has been put on a waiting list and you have been told you will probably have a date booked in three months' time. Write or tape how you would prepare your three-year-old child.

6 Brief: To develop a commercial product that would be an attractive alternative to the confectionery that most children eat

- What market research will you need to do?
- How can you keep production costs down?
- How would you advertise this product? (Don't forget the Advertising Standards).
- Should you organise a pilot evaluation?
- Should such products be clearly labelled with contents?

If this has been an interesting topic for you, try one of the following:

1 Experiment with inventing a savoury ice-lolly. If you can develop a really healthy and delicious one you may be able to make and sell some for a charity or school fête.

2 Find out if there is a correlation between the amount of sweets and chocolate eaten and tooth decay. If you're not sure what a correlation is read the assignment on pages 92–93.

3 Write a puppet play that would help very young children understand the importance of teeth-cleaning.

4 Answer this letter sent to a magazine for parents:

Dear Kate,

I really am trying to keep my child's teeth in good order. I insist she cleans her teeth after each meal, I cook healthy meals and have shown her how to use dental floss. My problem comes every day after school. All her friends are greeted with a bar of chocolate, an ice-lolly or a bag of crisps. She thinks I'm an ogre because I won't do this. Can you suggest what I should do?

Yours sincerely,
Mary Jones

7 Brief: To devise a way of assisting a parent to cope with a baby during a flight with a commercial airline

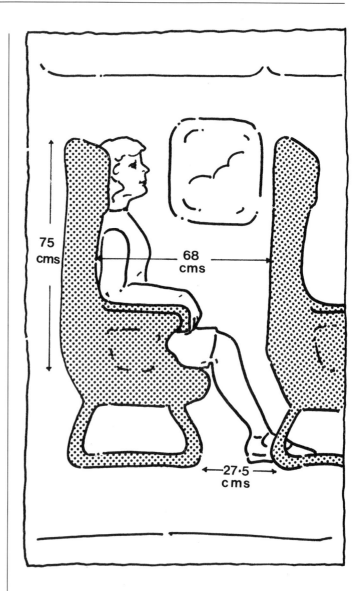

- How can you find out what exactly are the problems with managing a baby during a flight?
- What is available already?
- Will the safety regulations on board affect your ideas?

If you want further work to do with this topic:

1 Make a list of the possible problems that might occur when taking a baby on holiday to a hot country.

2 Design and make a flight play kit for either 2–5-year-olds or 5–8-year-olds. The pack should fit into an A4 envelope.

3 Design and make a flight meal, prepackaged as the adult ones, but made attractive for and suitable to the needs of toddlers.

4 Make a list of the advantages and disadvantages of travelling with small children by car, rail or coach.

8 Brief: To develop an artefact that would help a child prepare for in-patient hospital treatment involving surgery

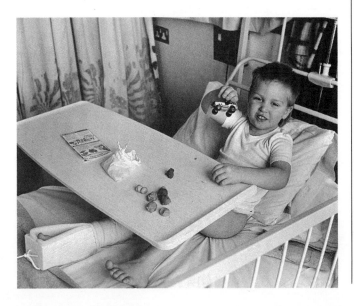

- What will the child need to understand?
- What's available already?
- Is honesty the best policy?

For you to try some more work connected with this topic:

1 How should parents help children to understand a divorce situation? Should the children be prepared for the separation? Should they be kept out of it? Write or record what you feel about it.
2 Write a poem about something that you were very upset about as a young child.
3 Find out what hospital treatments were like a 100 years ago.
4 Make a list of the personal qualities a children's nurse would need to make a success of her/his career.

9 Brief: To devise a way of helping to reduce the number of children killed or seriously injured on the roads

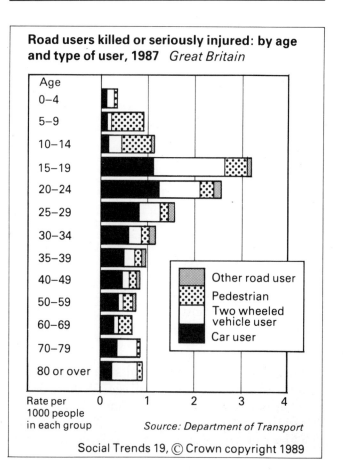

Road users killed or seriously injured: by age and type of user, 1987 *Great Britain*

Rate per 1000 people in each group

Source: Department of Transport

Social Trends 19, © Crown copyright 1989

Putting safety first

Adult casualties may have fallen but more children than ever are being killed on Britain's roads

During the late 1950s about 1,500 young teenagers were killed or badly injured on the roads in Britain every year. By 1984 the toll had doubled. These figures and the masking of their relentless rise will be raised at a European Road Safety Year conference at Guildhall, City of London, today by Frank West-Oram, vice-chairman of the Pedestrians' Association.

"This killing of children is a national disaster but it is obscured by the decline in road casualties as a whole", he says. "Among reasons for that general decline are stronger cars, the wearing of seat belts and less walking. The result is that people think the roads are safer, although for pedestrians they are becoming more and more dangerous."

The Department of Transport is aware of these facts. David Smith, head of road safety, said earlier this year that the decline in casualties among motorists "seems likely to leave pedestrians the largest single road-user casualty group in the 1990s".

Peter Bottomley, Minister for Roads, has gone further than any of his predecessors in advising road safety engineers to switch their attention from vehicles to people. "A third of all journeys are made entirely on foot. Most other journeys involve walking to some degree. That must make pedestrians the most important class of road user. Too often planners seem to forget that", he said in April. But no successful action for reducing

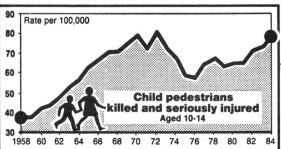

Rate per 100,000

Child pedestrians killed and seriously injured Aged 10-14

1958 60 62 64 66 68 70 72 74 76 78 80 82 84

teenage casualties has yet been taken.

"The first priority is to do something about the speed at which drivers travel in towns", Mr West-Oram said. "We know from the work of Professor Ian Howarth at the University of Nottingham that casualties occur in residential areas because drivers ignore children and not the other way round. We need to narrow the roads and use sleeping policemen to slow down cars", he said.

"The Pedestrians' Association wants to see better policing and improved driver training as well. In Norway you get a driving licence only after passing two tests. You receive a provisional licence after the first but it is made permanent only after another test, a year later. Something

similar should be introduced for new drivers in Britain."

Reducing casualties among the 10-14s presents special difficulties. Such children are beginning to explore on their own and tend to give up the "Green Cross Code" ritual.

They learn to cross the roads by copying adults. In time most successfully master the dangerous trick of choosing a gap in the traffic, aiming for the rear bumper of the car ahead of it, and marching into the road.

Before the year is over about 3,000 young boys and girls will fail this test. They will be killed or hurt. To some extent this is not surprising, since nowhere are children taught that the way most adults cross the roads is both difficult and stupid.

Terence Bendixson

- Which groups are most at risk?
- Should you concentrate on the children or the dangerous environment?

Further work on this topic:
1 How many people take risks on the roads around your school or college? Write notes of how the risks of your school/college environment could be reduced.
2 How can you show your sympathy to someone who has lost a close relative as a result of a road accident?
3 Role-play two friends. One of the pair has had quite a lot of alcoholic drink and is saying that he intends driving home in that state. The other person is trying to persuade him not to.
4 Plan an assembly for a primary school to warn the children of the danger they are in from cars and other traffic.

10 Brief: To devise a way of transporting a toddler over very rough and overgrown terrain

```
                                    18 Cavendish Court,
                                    Leith Road,
                                    Edinburgh.

                                    14th May 1989
```

Dear Tom,

        Thank you for your letter.
        I've decided to take both the children on our expedition. I can
almost hear you groaning. I've thought through the alternatives and
really have decided that we must bring Jamie and Duncan if Sally is to
be our 4th team member.
        Jamie is no real problem. He's 12 now and very fit and strong.
He's trekked with us before and I know he's capable of being quite a
useful member of the team. It's Duncan who'll be more of a problem.
He's three now and will not be able to walk for any distance in the
heat through that terrain. Luckily the plan is to make quite short
treks between camps – it's how we transport him? The terrain is
particularly rough and overgrown. We'll need to have some sort of
transportation that will cope with this.
        See you on the 26th. We'll talk more then.

                                    Yours,
                                    David.

- It would be good if your idea also helped with the heat problem.
- Does it make a difference to your design if the expedition is a short or a long one?
- Can you make adaptations to an existing child transporter?

Some further ideas to work on:

1 How could you keep Duncan happy during his time in the transporter? Write or record your ideas. Then find out from another student what she/he thinks of them. Improve your ideas after this talk.

2 Have you ever had a really adventurous holiday? Tell someone else about it.

3 Design and make an artefact for keeping food safe and fresh whilst on an expedition such as David's.

4 Write a storybook to prepare Duncan for the expedition. He has never been on one before, knows nothing about tents, campfires, no toilets, etc. Your book ought to make him look forward to the adventure.

11 Brief: To develop an artefact or system that would help to alleviate the problem of easy credit allowing families to slip into debt situations that have serious implications for the children

Easy credit 'destroying families through debt'

By Ruth Gledhill

Easy credit is allowing families to slip into debt, with wives and children suffering most, according to a report published yesterday by the Women's National Commission.

Families simply do not have enough money to make ends meet and few realize that their house can be repossessed for a debt of as little as £1,000.

It has become socially acceptable to be overdrawn but the end result is often divorce and lost homes.

The commission, which is an advisory body to the Government and is chaired by Mrs Angela Rumbold, the Minister of State for Education and Science, wants tighter controls on moneylenders, better education for the public, especially school-leavers, on how to budget and the reinstatement of a minimum deposit in credit agreements.

Miss Shirley Rolfe, secretary to the working party, said: "We hope to draw the Government's attention to the growing problem of debt in this country.

"We hope the Government will act on the recommendations we have made. They could alleviate the problem in future years."

The working party took advice from the National Association of Citizens' Advice Bureaux, the Office of Fair Trading and a trading standards officer.

It was particularly concerned with women who get caught up in the spiral of "robbing Peter to pay Paul".

The report blames changes in social attitudes, the wide and easy availability of credit, sudden drops in income and low income generally for the increasing debt problem.

"Consumers are bombarded daily with advertisements, in the press, on television and through the post, encouraging them to take out personal loans and store cards", the report says. "The consumer is made to feel unsophisticated if he or she does not use credit."

- Do the general public understand the possible results of getting into debt?
- Are young people being educated about the credit facilities that will be available to them as young adults?
- Do we want a society where we have winners and losers?
- What is being done now to help people who get into debt with easy credit?

Further work on this topic:

1 Write a description of how you would feel if your family had to live in one small room.

2 'Never a borrower nor a lender be' is an old saying that some people still believe in. Write or record your opinion of this idea.

3 Find out, by writing to them, what the policies of the major credit card companies are concerning the young customer.

4 Write a pamphlet that could be distributed through the library service explaining the dangers of borrowing money from a 'loan shark'.

12 Brief: To design a game or activity that would help the pre-school child acquire and develop the pre-reading skills they need before they can learn to read

Why don't you need all of this writing to be able to read it?

Mu name ir Tannie

Fill in the missing letters:

Once upon a . . . ., there were three little . . . . Their names were Isabel,

Davinder and Anita. They lived in a . . . . . with four bedrooms. The house was by

the . . . . . . This was lovely for the . . . ., it meant that they could go

swimming every day in the . . . .

How were you able to do that?

What do you need to be able to do before you could successfully do that?

Riddle

Q. When is a bicycle not a bicycle ?

A. When it is a Bicycle or a BICYCLE .

What games help you to learn to match shapes?

Can you read the following two passages?

air the into up thrown was ball the
river the near trees some by fell and
to hoping it get to rushed children The
Sound and safe it Find

allowed	always	She	her	that	ago
to	was	was	than	Jane	years
stay	he	very	younger	found	six
up	because	cross	was	out	was
late.	this	about	Jim	that	It

Which way do we read written English? (Usually, that is.)

- How can you find out more about the skills you need before you can read?
- At what age do children usually acquire these skills?
- Can you design an activity that will help develop one or more pre-reading skills?
- Are pre-reading skills the same whatever language the child is going to learn to read?

Further work you could try if you have enjoyed this topic:

1   How can parents help their children to be 'ready to read'. Write or record your ideas. You might like to try and produce a pamphlet for parents on the subject.

2   How do deaf children manage to acquire pre-reading skills? Make a list of those they would find difficult. Perhaps you could invite a teacher of deaf children to visit your class and explain how deaf children are helped with their language development.

3   Draw a picture and colour it. Make it easy for a child to see all the things in it. Could a child make up a story about the picture? Try it out on a three-year-old child.

4   Find out what your local children's library provides for children who cannot read. Make notes of what you discover.

PART
3

Methodology

Methodological assignments

1 Making comparisons

We make comparisons all the time in our everyday lives. When we go shopping to buy clothes, sports gear, household and electrical goods and music tapes and discs, we make comparisons in order to choose which item among many would best suit us. There is even an organisation called the Consumers Association that publishes a guide to choice by making detailed comparison between different makes of the same item.

If you listen to parents talking about their young children, they will often compare notes about how their offspring are getting on. So you hear:

'Mine's got two teeth now, how many has yours?'

'Is your child still having difficulty managing to feed herself?'

'She reads quite well now. What book is he on?'

'Is your son potty-trained? Mine is still refusing to oblige.'

'She got six gold stars last week, how many did your daughter get?'

We often make comparisons to be reassured or to confirm a problem.

Some comparisons are made to impress people. To try and prove that someone or something is better in some way or another. Sometimes simple statistics are used to impress us. This technique is often used by advertisers who want us to buy their products. For example, 85 per cent of mothers who chose FLASHGATE toothpaste said their children had no fillings.

People often make unfair comparison. A skilled investigator tries very hard to be fair when making comparisons.

These are the GCSE results of two different schools in different parts of the country.

At first glance it looks as if St Glorious is the school to go to if you want good GCSE results. As a class, think of some reasons why this comparison might not be a fair one. **Consider** these points:

1   How many pupils were involved? Suppose St Glorious only allowed ten of their best pupils to sit the exams, whereas Honesty Lane school had a policy that all pupils were entered for all the subjects they had studied for?

2   Do the schools have the same amount of money to spend on learning materials, number of teachers, equipment, etc? Might that make a difference that cannot be reflected in those simple statistics?

3   Are the figures reflecting the same measure?

Suppose Honesty Lane school considers a pass to be a grade C and above whereas St Glorious considers a pass to be all graded entrants?

Do you think it might affect the results if one of these schools was situated in a very deprived inner city environment?

Does wealth buy good results?

Some unfair comparisons can be damaging to children's welfare and often research methods are questioned. *How* you find things out can be as important as *what* you find out.

One comparison you might want to make one day, if you have a child of your own, would be to compare two or more infant schools. How would you tackle that task? How could you make it a fair comparison? One way would be to make some decisions before you visited the schools about:

(a) what you would expect to be able to observe for yourself;

(b) what answers you would hope for to certain questions you would want to ask the headteacher.

In a small group, **write** a checklist of the things you would expect to see or hear on a visit to an infant school. You can also **generate** a few questions you would want to ask the headteacher. Note down what answers you would hope to get with a reason for why you think that answer would be the best.

Think of strategies that you could use to improve your checklist. For example, if you decide that you would expect an infant school to look colourful and visually interesting because you feel that children will learn from looking and discussing what they see, you might find that both or all the infant schools have displays on the walls, but some are more successful than others. To improve the straight checklist you could add a simple rating scale and add a chance to jot down a comment or two.

Item to be rated	Rating			Comments
School A Wall displays	+	✓	−	Mostly children's work – some dated over a year ago.
School B Wall displays	✓			Very creative. Full of life. Obviously children's own work. Watched a group of 6 yr olds putting up a display of their work in science.
School C Wall displays			✓	Only posters and teacher instructions. Very boring to look at.

However, it could be that different children need different types of schools. **Read** these descriptions of two girls both aged 4¾. The descriptions are written by their mothers.

> Rachael is a quiet and sensible child. She tires easily and is often quite frightened of perfectly harmless things. It took months of reassurance to allay her fear of a cartoon character on the TV. Even now she will seek my company when this character appears on the screen. I think she's going to be quite talented artistically, she spends most of her playing time drawing and pattern-making. Even in the garden or on the beach she makes pattern pictures with leaves, twigs, seeds, stones, shells and seaweed. She is able to concentrate for ages and when other children come to play they get cross because she often seems locked into her own world rather than theirs. She's a fussy eater and always inspects what I give her to eat. Any blemish on a piece of fruit will lead her to reject it. She is a great observer, often telling me, in full detail, about things that happened days ago. She gets very embarrassed if I tell her that she's made a mistake, her eyes fill with tears and she looks frightened. I've tried to reassure her about this, but it still happens.

> Denise is a handful. She's very lively and seems to have so much energy. She loves physical activities and is already very good at climbing, cartwheels, jumping, swimming and balancing. She is always laughing and hardly ever complains about anything. She can be disobedient – if you tell her to do something, she gives me a look as if to say, 'Try and make me – it might be fun.' She really enjoys new experiences – even her first visit to the dentist. She never stops talking. As she plays she produces a running commentary on the activity. She does quieten down when I read to her, but directly the story is over, she's up and acting out the story, making me take part as one of the characters. Luckily she sleeps like a log and eats anything I put in front of her. She's extremely fond of chocolate and I have to take care that she doesn't get overweight. Other children are her best playthings, she tends to get bored on her own.

In your groups **decide** whether these children need different qualities in an infant school. Make a list of what each child is going to need if they are going to be happy and learn well at infant school.

Depending on what course you are studying at school/college it might be possible for some or all of you to actually visit an infant school. If you can, then you could test your checklist for real. If you do this you should also find time to discuss with your group how useful the list was and whether you would need to improve it in some way.

You could practice making comparisons by doing one of the following:

1   Make a list of criteria you could use when choosing an item of clothing for yourself. Compare your list with one made by someone else. How did they vary? Why did they vary?
2   Compare your handwriting with a friend's. Make sure the comparison is as fair as possible. Write down how you made the comparison fair. What factors about the handwriting did you use in the comparison?
3   Look in magazines and newspapers or on TV for examples of comparative statistics being used to impress people. Choose one to decide what else you need to know before you are impressed.
4   Compare two buildings designed for the same purpose. Decide which one is best serving its purpose.

2 Correlations

What is a correlation?

A correlation is a *link* between two different factors.

Examples

About two decades ago doctors found a correlation between smoking tobacco and lung cancer. They found that there seemed to be a definite link between the two things. They found that the more tobacco people smoked the more likely they were to develop lung cancer.

At about the same time, a researcher looking at delinquency in adolescents found a correlation between street lights and delinquency. The researcher found that the more street lights there were the higher the rate of juvenile delinquency.

In spite of a clear link between the two things, a correlation does not necessarily prove that one thing is causing the other.

For instance, in the first example there could be another factor that causes people to smoke and to get lung cancer later in life. That other factor could be 'city living'. It could be that living in a city is more stressful and causes people to turn to smoking as a way of relieving that stress. It could be that the air pollution in a city is the cause of lung cancer. Often the finding of a strong correlation between two factors serves as a starting point for further research that finds out whether one thing is causing the other. In the example about smoking, the research has continued and more and more evidence has been found to make doctors convinced that smoking *is* one of the major causes of lung cancer.

Do you think the high number of street lights causes delinquency? Or is there another factor influencing both of those things? **Discuss** with a partner what you think.

Try some more. Are the following correlations the result of cause and effect or not?
1 The more stressful a job is, the more likelihood of having a heart attack.
2 The better the parents' musical ability the more likelihood there is of having a very musical child.
3 The bigger the home the better the likelihood of having more personal possessions.
4 The earlier a child learns to read the better the success in GCSE at 16.

How do you find out if there is a correlation between two things?

One simple way of investigating whether factors are correlated is to do a scattergram.

Example

To find out whether there is a correlation between intelligence and success in examinations at 16.

Measures used were intelligence tests and number of GCSE passes graded at C or above. *Method*: Using the members of one class of 30 students, at the end of the summer term after the examinations had been completed but before leaving school the students were given an intelligence test. Their exam results were noted when they arrived from the examination board.

Data

Boys	IQ	No. of exams at C or above	Girls	IQ	No. of exams at C or above
1	100	5	1	96	4
2	120	4	2	126	5
3	115	4	3	132	4
4	110	3	4	114	3
5	110	7	5	120	4
6	130	7	6	113	1
7	135	5	7	100	0
8	106	3	8	102	0
9	108	3	9	116	6
10	102	2	10	120	6
11	112	1	11	106	4
12	110	0	12	110	2
13	100	2	13	101	1
14	98	1			
15	95	0			
16	140	3			
17	111	1			

Make a scattergram

Put one of the measures on each axis. Make sure you have enough room on each scale for the full range of scores on both factors. Make sure you space the scales into equal divisions. In this case the range of scores are:

    Intelligence test: 95–140
    No. of GCSEs at C and above: 0–7

Now look at each person's results and plot them on the scattergram.

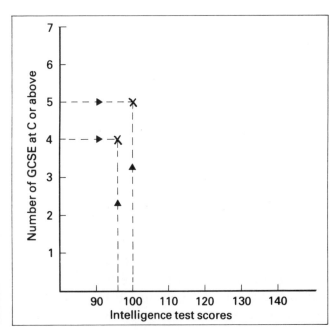

Take no. 1 boy, find 100 on your scale and draw a line upwards until you reach level 5 GCSEs. Mark the spot with a small clear cross. For no. 1 girl you will start at 96 and go up to 4.

Now complete your own scattergram for this class of pupils.

When you have finished, compare the pattern of small crosses on your scattergram with these:

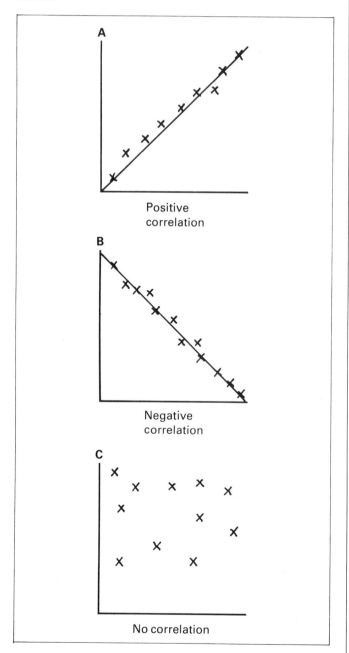

If your scattergram looks like C, then there is no correlation between the intelligence of the pupils and their GCSE results. If that were to be true, your scattergram would look like A.

However, if it looked like B it would mean that the more intelligent a pupil is the poorer her/his GCSE results would be. A is called a positive correlation; B is called a negative correlation.

Are you surprised by the results in this example? Can you think of some reasons why this might happen?

You can only do correlation studies when using factors that can be put on a scale.

Try a correlation study with your class members. Choose one of the following:
1   The taller you are the more you weigh.
2   The quicker your handwriting is the more likely it is to be untidy. (This will need some careful thought about the measures you use.)
3   The more chocolate you eat the fatter you are.
4   The bigger your triceps muscle is the better you are at throwing a ball a long distance.

3 Observing children

Observing children accurately is a difficult skill. It is not easy to be with children *and* observe carefully what they are doing and how they react to the activity. If you have ever been to a nursery, a playgroup or a home where there are young children, you will know that the children will often stop what they are doing in order to investigate the person (you) who has just arrived. Sometimes they are shy and seek the protective closeness of the parent or teacher when other adults come into their world.

Young children often have very short spans of concentration, so that they seem to do many different things in a short space of time.

Read this observation made by a student studying a boy, aged three years one month, playing in the kitchen whilst his mother cleared away the breakfast things. His eighteen-month-old sister was sitting in her high-chair in the same room. The boy is referred to as J, the mother as M and the sister as R. There are many different ways of recording an observation. This student chose to record her observations using three columns.

Time	Action	Language
8.15.01	J got down from table, spilling orange juice on to cloth.	M: Oh dear. J: Dear.
8.15.06	J tipped toy box out all over floor, mostly under R's chair. Lifts teddy from floor, holds tight to chest, puts head on one side. Spies jigsaw piece in corner by window.	J: Cars coming . . . come . . . teddy . . . J: Do jigsaw.
8.15.08	Roots around in amongst all the toys piled up under the high-chair. R drops spoon on J's head.	M: Find all the pieces then. J: [Yells]
8.15.09	J hits R with teddy. Drops teddy. Moves over to M at sink. J puts hands into the washing-up water. Lifts down two hands-full of detergent bubbles.	J: R . . . spoon on my head. M: Poor you. R . . . I'll get you out in a sec.
8.15.20	Rushes around room making car noises and blowing little bits of foamy bubbles into the air.	
8.15.32	Sits down on floor by window, slightly hidden from M's view. Wipes the rest of foam on to the window pane and spreads it about. Blows on it. Laughs.	M: What's so funny?
8.15.40	J looking for something on floor. Sees a yellow plastic brick. Reaches out for it and then uses it to press on to the wet window pane. Moves it around making more car noises. R also making car noises.	

All that happened in *less than a minute*.

In your small group:
1 **Decide** what you have learned about J and his family from this very short observation. Make a list.
2 Decide what the observer needed to do and have with them in order to do this observation. **Record** your ideas.
3 **List** the skills demonstrated by this observer.

Join up with another small group to **share** what you decided and discuss the following points:
* Why do you think that observations might be a useful way of studying children?
* Is it better to observe children in surroundings familiar to them? What do you think? What are your reasons?

Share your thoughts with the whole class.

Back in your small group, work out a way of developing the skills needed to be able to observe accurately. **Plan** an activity for the rest of your class to do. The activity should be to help your fellow students develop one or more of the skills needed for observation work. You should design your activity to last no more than five minutes. It might be a practise observation, a game or some other way of practicing looking carefully, listening accurately or recording clearly. You will need to plan this activity carefully, being quite clear about what you need to do to make it work. This is a technological activity and you will need time to do it well.

When all the groups have carried out their activities, you will need some time to **discuss** how well they achieved their purpose. Were they a fun way of developing skills?

If time allows you could choose one of the following to do:
1 Design a way of recording an observation of a child for an observer who finds it difficult to write quickly.

2   Observe a fellow student for at least a minute. Record exactly what they did. This is best done without them knowing.

3   List all the sounds you can hear both inside and outside the room that you are working in. Only record those sounds you can actually hear. These take a minute or two to really concentrate upon, then you should hear many different noises.

4   Decide how an observer of children can get over the problem of the observer's presence changing the situation that might have occurred if the observer had not been present. Are there any ways around this problem?

4 Writing a case study

How does a case study differ from an observation? Look at the observation on page 95 and the case study of Genie on page 12. In a small group decide which one is which:

A
- Might deal with a long span of time and a particular situation.
- Makes judgements based upon the information stated.
- Deals with a variety of types of information.
- Sometimes contains B.

B
- Deals with a short time span.
- Makes no judgements.
- Gives a precise type of information.

In a small group **decide** why a case study must be recorded in a very sensitive way that has the child's welfare as a priority.

Think about what you might feel if a case study was written about you. What would you want to be sure about before you gave permission for it to be done? **Discuss** this in your group.

Are there any ways of making the subject of a case study less vulnerable?

Read the following extracts from case studies. Decide which demonstrate that the writer might not have thought about the best interests of the child concerned.

'Jane Dodds of 17 Downberry Drive, Woodford Green, Essex, is 6 years and 3 months old. She was born to an unmarried mother at Leyton Green Hospital after a Caesarian section operation.'

'J, now aged 3½, was born in Scotland to a mother infected with HIV. Until she was seven months old J developed normally and appeared to be a thoroughly healthy and well-nourished child. In her eighth month, her mother noticed J's disinclination to remain sitting up in her pram. On consultation with the specialist doctor, J was diagnosed as HIV-infected.'

'This 15-year-old girl is in moral danger. She stays out late at night, has managed to get a prescription for contraceptive pills. She dresses like a tart and it is no wonder that her parents are at their wits end.'

'C has difficulty in learning. She has been recommended for an intellectual assessment which will be done in about two months' time. Meanwhile, her obviously low intelligence is hampering her development as well as those other children in the class.'

'On visiting his home, it was typical of a family of that culture, the boys being thoroughly spoiled whilst the girls are doing all of the work.'

'Louise has many toys. Unfortunately most of them are broken or have essential pieces missing. If a system for keeping them in a better state could be devised, she would benefit from the many different activities the toys would provide.'

Write a list of the Dos and Don'ts when writing a case study.

Display yours and read other groups' work.

Study the following case study, written by a teacher for a social worker. The social worker requested the case study as part of her investigation into the family circumstances. She asked the teacher to provide an overview of this eight-year-old boy.

Case study

This boy has been in my class for nearly a whole school year. I did have some dealings with him for part of last year when he attended the modelling club I run during Thursday lunchtimes. He is of average ability overall. He is rather better at mathematical, scientific and technological than language skills. He is able to read and write at a level of competence one would expect from a seven-year-old. He shows a creative flair when tackling problems and at such times tends to become the leader of the group of children he works with.

He always arrives at school looking clean and suitably dressed for the weather. He makes his own way home to the Pendlebury Estate, which is about half a mile from the school. He eats a school lunch daily and usually heads the queue for second helpings of both courses. In spite of this he is a thin and spindly child with below-average physical abilities. He runs in an unco-ordinated fashion, is unable to climb a rope and shows poor balance on the apparatus. He enjoys football and swimming and is making slow progress in both. His behaviour is generally good although he can get over-excited at times. On the whole he is quieter than most of the other boys in my class and tends to keep a low profile in large group situations. I have only met one of his parents - his father came to the school about four months ago after an episode when his son's blazer was torn during a scuffle in the playground. Neither parent has attended any school functions in spite of many invitations to events such as open evenings, sports day and the school concert. I have noticed him occasionally annoying other pupils by quietly taking away something they need to do the task I have set them. It is not that he needs the object, he just hides it away from those who do. During this year he has had two hearing tests. The first showed a possible minimal hearing loss, the second was normal. He shows very little interest in music or drawing, but enjoys needlework activities.

Decide, as a group, whether this case study gives you an overall view of this child.

Check with your Dos and Don'ts. Has the teacher got the best interests of this child in mind, do you think?

What parts do you think the social worker will be particularly interested in?

If you want some further work to do, choose one of the following:

1   Write a case study about yourself. The case study could be used to help your school write your school-leaving report.

2   Look at one of the other case studies in this book (pages 12–15). Decide whether it conforms to your list of Dos or Don'ts.

3   Read a book called *Dibs in Search of Self* by Virginia Axline (Penguin, 1964). This whole book is a case study about a young child. You will certainly be able to borrow this book from a public library if there is not a copy in school.

4   Write a case study of a child portrayed in a TV soap opera.

5 Conducting a survey

'In tests, 8 out of 10 owners say their cat prefers . . . .'

Every ten years the government does a census of the population, but more often a general household survey is done. This is to find out many different things about how people live, what they do for a living, how many children are being born, and much more. It is from such a survey that simple statistical statements can be made. Such as:

'The average family in the UK contains 2¼ children.'

'7% of the households have a dishwasher.'

'96% of the households own or rent a TV.'

'The average 16 year old in England and Wales is awarded 3.4 GCSE grades.'

Doing a survey is a way of finding out what is the most usual. They tend to be quantitive investigations that produce numerical data.

Have you ever been stopped in the street by someone doing a survey?

Did you know that is how the media find out which TV programmes are the most popular? They ask a large number of people what they watched on a certain day. As long as they ask enough people of different ages, occupations and in different parts of the country, they can calculate roughly how many people must have watched each programme.

Have you ever watched the progress of a general election on TV?

Often they choose a constituency that is likely to be typical of the whole country, do a pre-election survey and then predict who is going to win the election. They usually get an extremely accurate prediction.

Marketing in industry is based on the idea that if you ask enough people some well-chosen questions you can generate enough information to be able to predict trends in buying and future demands, and so redesign advertising to target particular groups of people. The next time you are watching the adverts on TV see if you can decide who is being targeted – the young, the old, the rich, the not-so-rich.

In groups, **list** as many ways as you can for *how* surveys are conducted. Have you ever conducted a survey as part of your studies? If you have, you will be able to contribute the difficulties you had with doing it.

Read this description of a survey made in a school.

A deputation of pupils went to their headteacher asking that the school uniform be abolished. These pupils felt that the school uniform was 'old-fashioned, unbecoming, expensive compared to other clothing, uncomfortable, sexist and it restricted individual development'.

The headteacher discussed this request with the staff and governors of the school who decided to let the parents decide.

All pupils were given a questionnaire to take home for their parent/s. The parents were asked:

Please tick your preference:
1   To retain the school uniform as it is for all pupils.
2   To abolish the school uniform for all pupils.
3   To retain the school uniform for the younger pupils only.
4   To redesign the school uniform to one more acceptable to all pupils.
Please add any reasons for your choice or comments you would like to make. Return to the school secretary by 1 May 1988.

This survey revealed the following information:

> (a) Of those parents who returned the form, 98 per cent were in favour of abolishing the school uniform.
> (b) 1 per cent wanted to retain the uniform for younger pupils only.
> (c) 1 per cent wanted to change the design of the school uniform to make it acceptable to all pupils.
>
> There were 1400 pupils in the school. 28 per cent of the parents completed the survey. Five parents added comments to the form they returned to the school secretary.

In your group, **discuss**:
- What would you have done if you had been the headteacher looking at the results of the survey?
- Why do you think only 392 parents responded?
- Should any other people have been asked for their views?

Decide how that survey might have been better conducted.

Design a survey to find out how much pocket money children should be given. Remember to consider *how* it should be conducted, *who* should be included, how the information gained should be processed and communicated.

When you have done this and shared your ideas about how best to produce a good survey, you might like to actually conduct it to see what you would find out.

Further ideas to work on are:
1 Go to the library and look at a journal called *Social Trends*. It is full of up-to-date information about social conditions and you should find some of the information very interesting.
2 Search through newspapers and magazines for results of recent surveys or for requests for information for a survey. Display the cuttings you find.
3 Write a letter to your careers officer asking for information about the qualifications needed and job opportunities in the market research business.
4 Draw a cartoon depicting a particularly bizarre statistical finding.

6 Interviewing people

In groups of *three* people with equal numbers of A and B groups (see below), **role-play** the three A or B interviewing situations. One person should act the role of the interviewer, one the person being interviewed and the third should take on the role of observer. Everyone should have a go at each role. After four minutes you should change to the next situation and take a different role.

The observer's job is to be the timekeeper and to note down what they observe from the interview.

'A' situations
A policewoman interviewing the parent of a missing child.
A secret police officer interviewing someone under suspicion of helping an escaped prisoner.
A TV presenter interviewing a well-known personality.

'B' situations
A doctor interviewing a patient.
An employer interviewing a school-leaver for a job vacancy.
A welfare officer interviewing a parent about the non-attendance at school of her/his child.

When you have had a go at each role, spend some time discussing the differences between those mini-interviews you have role-played.
- How did they make you feel?
- Who did most of the talking?
- Did the person being interviewed have time to think?
- Were the questions clear?
- Did the questions follow on in a logical order?
- How did the mood of the interviewer affect the answers given by the person being interviewed?

Think about the following situation:

A social scientist is doing some research into the sexual behaviour of young people. She needs information from the young people themselves. Decide whether she will get better information by interviewing them or sending a questionnaire to complete.

Make a list of the advantages and disadvantages to her research of an interview approach. Do this on a large sheet of paper so that you can easily share your thoughts with the rest of the class.

Consider the role of an interviewer. First, make a list of all the things an interviewer would need to plan before the interview takes place; eg, does it make a difference *where* the interview is held?

Supposing some research requires several people to be interviewed to find out their views and experiences on the same topic. Does it make a difference if:
- It is the same person who interviews each person?
- The interviewer is of the opposite sex?
- The interviewer is dressed in really casual clothes?
- The interviewer is in a hurry?

Do you think the person interviewing could affect what people say to her/him? **Note** down how the interviewer should conduct an interview to get the fairest results.

Sometimes researchers use a technique whereby, instead of doing the interview themselves, they employ another carefully chosen person to do it for them. This is to prevent the researcher influencing the results of the investigation. The researcher has often got clear ideas of what she/he thinks the interviewees are going to say. To avoid interpreting what is actually said in a way that matches those preconceived ideas the employed interviewer who stands in for the researcher is not told what the researcher is trying to find out.

What is the best way to record an interview?

As a group, **list** all the possible ways this could be done. Note the advantages and disadvantages of each method. **Display** your work and check on what other groups decided.

To practice some of the skills involved in interviewing, choose one of the following to try:

1   Prepare an interview schedule for finding out about the dreams people have. If you can, use one of your fellow students to find out if it enabled them to talk comfortably about their dreams.
2   Record an interview using one of the methods you discussed in your group. Did you record the interview word for word?
3   Make a list of all the people you might interview if you were researching sleep problems in children under the age of five years. Note your reasons.
4   Imagine that you have been given the job of designing a room to be used solely for the purpose of interviewing distressed children. Write notes of what you think the room should be like and why. You may want to draw some of these notes.

7 Taking measurements

Quantitative measures are objective and should be the same whoever does the measuring. Look at the picture on page xx.

Make a similar **list** of quantitative measures that can be done on parenthood.

What about qualitative measures? These are subjective and likely to vary according to who is making the judgements.

For example, can you measure how happy a child is? How well they are learning? How helpful they are? How musical they are?

Think about 'happiness'.
- What behaviour would we expect from a friend who feels happy? Or especially happy?
- Have you ever seen anyone who is so happy that they cry or cuddle a complete stranger? What about beauty contests; doesn't the winner always cry?
- Are there individual differences in how people show their feelings?
- Are there cultural differences in how people express their feelings?
- What behaviour would you expect from someone who is unhappy?
- Would it vary according to their age?
- Would it vary according to their sex?
- How do we know when we see someone cry whether they are just a little unhappy or utterly miserable? Or are they weeping for joy?

How can happiness or unhappiness be measured?

How tall a child is
How heavy a child is
What shape they are
How many teeth they have
How big their feet are
How fast they can run
How high they can climb
How long they can concentrate
How many words they understand
How many words they can read
How far they can jump
How far they can swim
What number they can count up to
How many letters they can identify
How big a breath they can take
How long they can hold their breath
How big is their stride
How far they can walk
How big is their hand span
How fast they can do their shoes up
How much they eat
How often they go to the lavatory
How quickly they are growing
How often they have an accident
How quickly their heart beats

Note your ideas and share them with another group. Add or subtract any of your original ideas that you wish to change as a result of this discussion.

As a whole class, **brainstorm** how you can measure a successful person. When you have generated as many ideas as you can, go over them deciding which are quantitative and which are qualitative.

Can you measure a 'successful child' using the same measures?

What would you add or subtract from your list?

The National Curriculum has been introduced into the state schools of the United Kingdom. Children and young adults will all receive a similar package of learning throughout the country. This includes children between the ages of 5–16 years. Children's progress is to be measured at 7, 11, 14 and 16 years. At 7 years old they will be assessed on targets in English, Maths and Science.

In your small group, **think** about the following issues in connection with measuring the abilities of children of this age:

- Will children feel failures if they do not reach the targets set?
- How will parents use the information they are given about the progress their children have made?
- Are there some circumstances in children's lives that will affect their performance at school and therefore the results of this assessment?
- Will children from multilingual homes be given credit for their abilities in more than one language?
- How can these assessments help children of this age?

Feedback your group's ideas to the whole class.

Do one of the following, either as an individual or with a partner:

1 Find out the average height of the students in your class. Remember that accuracy is a vital part of the skill of measuring. You could also draw a histogram to show the difference in height between the boys and girls.

Dear Mrs. Jones,

I was rather worried to hear from Claire's Teacher that she is progressing rather slowly in English although she is average in Maths and Science.

Could you please advise me on how I could help her to improve her language skills.

I think she is too young for homework, but there must be ways of encouraging her reading and writing in fun ways.

Yours sincerely
Janet Burden (mother of Claire Burden in 2c)

2 Answer the above letter to a head-teacher from a parent of a 7-year-old child attending her school.

3 Mrs Jones, the headteacher of the Angel Primary School, wants to give a prize to the most helpful child in the school. Can you devise a fair way that would find the child who most deserved such a description? Write or record on tape your method.

4 Either, write a short description of the qualities you possess that are not measured by the examination system, or make a list of GCSE titles that you think would better suit your talents and skills. You could have a lot of fun with this task.

8 Writing an investigational report

This is not a difficult job as long as you have a clear idea of what you are trying to do.

An investigational report is a way of explaining your investigation to a reader, as if that reader is totally ignorant of the work you have been doing. If your report is to be assessed for an examination grade, then the examiner needs to know exactly what you were attempting to investigate; exactly how you went about it; what you found out; and what conclusions you made as a consequence. A final description of any flaws in the design and execution of your investigation will make the examiner understand that you have learned by your mistakes and will give you credit for it.

What goes where

Heading	What goes into this section
Purpose	This should contain a statement that describes what you have investigated. It is often in the form of a question; eg, Is it difficult to become a childminder? Sometimes the investigation is designed to question a statement; eg, 'It is harder to bring up a boy than a girl.' If you think it is important, you can describe your reasons for choosing to investigate this particular aspect of the subject. You cannot investigate a topic; eg, 'Nappies'. You can choose an aspect of that topic; eg, 'How much of the family budget is spent on buying disposable nappies?'. Or you could question the statement 'Disposable nappies are expensive'.
Clarification task	You cannot investigate the topic 'Adoption'. What aspect of the topic could you investigate?
Information/data sought	This section should contain exact details of the type of data you were trying to get. This doesn't mean copying out lots of information about the topic. It is not a background section. Of course, you will want to read around the topic area to clarify your ideas. You should only include in your report information that is needed in order to explain the type of information/data you were seeking. For example, suppose you were investigating the statement 'It is harder to bring up a boy than a girl' and you chose this because your granny believed this. You could include the information that you had looked in several books about bringing up children, but none had commented on the supposed difficulty in raising a boy.
Clarification task	Do this with a partner. **Fill in the gaps** in the chart.

Investigational purpose	Information/data/evidence sought
To question the statement 'Boys are harder to bring up than girls'.	Verbal opinions from parents of families that include children of both sexes.
Is it difficult to become a childminder?	
	Costs per week of disposable nappies. Family income per week. Obtained verbally from several families with one baby between 3–6 months and no other children who wear nappies.
To question the statement that children learn best if they have enough sleep.	

Method

This should include the exact details of how you obtained your data. For example, in the investigation to question the statement 'It is harder to bring up boys than girls' you would need to describe how many parents you sought opinions from; whether you asked only parents who had children of both sexes; whether you asked as many fathers as mothers; whether they were all asked in the same way; whether you used a questionnaire or interview; and whether the parents you asked were a typical cross-section of the general population; that is, did you include parents from different socio-economic groups, different cultural and ethnic backgrounds. These details help the reader to know whether your investigation is a fair one or not.

Clarification task

What methodological details would you need to include if you were writing a report on one of the other three investigations in the chart under 'Information data sought' clarification task? Do this task with a partner.

Results

In this section you explain what you found out by using the method described in the report. If your data is quantitative it is best to use a simplified expression of your findings by using a graph, chart or pictogram. If, however, your data is qualitative, you should write a summary of your main findings. The detail of the data can be included in an appendix to the report.

Clarification task

This is a list of the type of information/data that a group of students were seeking. Which ones are likely to produce quantitative data that can be displayed in graphical form?
   Comparing birthweights of newborn babies
   Children's opinions of TV
   Sizes of children's gardens in different areas of the same town
   Number of different types of play materials
   Teenagers' views on the responsibilities of parenthood
   Time spent on particular activities in a nursery
   Types of help for families in distress.

Conclusion

This is where you write what your results are telling you. For example, your results for 'Is it easy to become a childminder?' might lead you to conclude that it does seem quite easy – you would then give your reasons why you have decided that. These reasons must be based on the data you have collected, not from other sources of information. You might also find something in your results that surprises you. You might have found something out by accident; eg, that there is a shortage of childminders in your area that you had not realised when you started your investigation. Your results may not give you much concrete evidence to support a firm conclusion. Negative results are as valid as positive ones. You should not feel disappointed if your investigation produces inconclusive evidence. You should explain in your conclusion why it is that you cannot make a firm conclusion.

Clarification task

These are the results of an investigation to find out how much of the family budget is spent on buying disposable nappies.

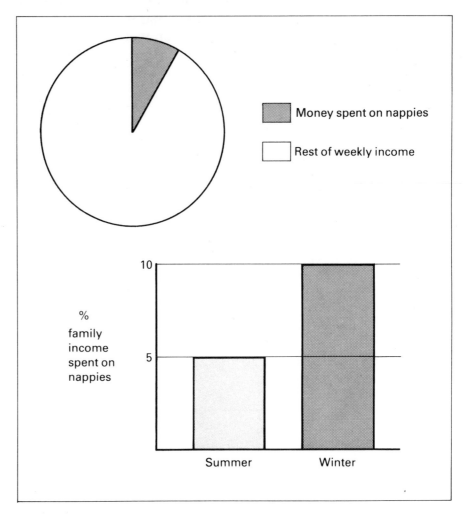

Work with a partner to decide what some of your conclusions might be.

Evaluation

This is your chance to be your own critic. Explain how you could have done the investigation better and why.

Clarification task

Work in a small group. Read the following investigation and complete the evaluation.

Purpose

To investigate how much attention is paid to the girls in a mixed class at the local primary school, where the class teacher is male. I decided to do this because I suspected that the girls are not being fairly treated.

Data sought

I am going to time how long the teacher spends attending to the girls compared with the boys. I shall time, using a stop-watch, any contact he has with any child, whether that is talking to them, watching what they are doing or helping them to do something.

Method

On three separate occasions I used a stop-watch to measure how much time was spent on the children in this class. Each time I did this for one hour. I recorded the time spent on girls in one column and that on the boys in another. Every time the teacher moved on to a different activity I reset the stop-watch.

Results

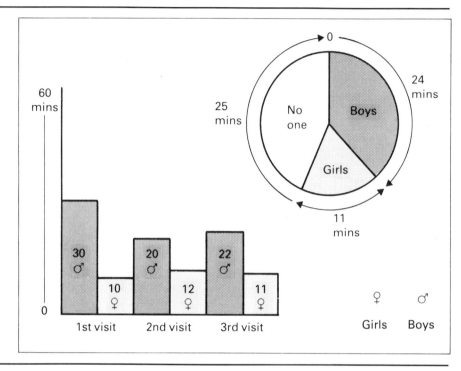

Conclusion

My results show that the teacher did indeed spend more time attending to the boys. I am not surprised because the boys seemed to demand more of him. They called out for him, asking for help and it was difficult for him not to respond. I was surprised at how much of the time the teacher was doing other things and not attending to the children. This time was mostly spent talking to people who came in to the room and sorting out books and papers.

Evaluation

You do this. But think very carefully about whether this student has given you enough information about the class.

In groups, use a copy of the following investigation done by another student. Cut, **rearrange** and stick on to a large sheet of paper this investigational report. Use the headings given in this assignment to sort out what she has written. Leave out any part that you think is irrelevant and note whether she has missed out anything of importance. If she has, perhaps you could put that right. **Share** your end-results with others in your class.

To practice the skills of writing clearly and informatively, try one of the following:

1 Write a report of an investigation you have done.
2 Write a clear and detailed description of the method by which you travel to school or college.
3 Evaluate your contribution to someone else's learning. This could be a friend, a younger family member or your class as a whole.
4 Write the purpose you have for *either* wearing the clothes you do *or* saving money every week.

Investigation

Introduction

My teacher says I've got to do an Investigation
for the exam. I thought a lot about what
I was gonna do because I hate writing.
I like doing quick things. I don't like doing
the same as everyone else. I think
Child Development is a nice lesson and I
love little kids. They are so cute.

I read in a book that if you smoke you have
little babies. When I told my mum about
this she says it isn't tru. My mum and my
big sister both smoke and they had very
big babies. I wayed reary ten pounds when
I was born and my little brother was just
under 11 pounds.

When a pregnant woman smokes, some of the
chemical substances in the smoke pass
from her lungs into the blood stream, and soon
reach the womb. At the placenta the
chemicals cross from the mothers blood
into the babys blood stream. They are then
carried to all parts of the babys body.
Two of the harmful chemicals in smoke
which reach the babys blood stream are
nicotine and carbon monoxide (the same
as poison as in car fumes).

What I did

I asked 10 mothers who smoke and 10 mothers who dont what they weight of there first baby was

1	4·2		1	7·11
2	5·7		2	7·2
3	8·2		3	5·1
4	7·1		4	6·0
5	5·8		5	8·7
6	6·3		6	7·6
7	6·6		7	7·3
8	7·0 (4)		8	7·6
9	6·1		9	7·3
10	6·9		10	7·9

10)62·10   10)70·8

6·4 ←——— Average ———→ 7·1

☒ Premature

What I found

My results show that the books are right. If you smoke during pregnancy it makes you have a smaller baby than if you dont.
I stood outside Sainsburys on a Saturday morning. I asked every woman who came along if they had a child. If they smoked and what there first child weiged. When I got 10 of each I stopped.

I wonder why the smoking didn't make me and my brother little. Maybe its to do with how many cigarets they smoke.
It might not be anything to do with smoking. It could be because I live in Kilburn it just happened that I asked posh people who dont smoke and poorer people who do. Maybe it was to do with having proper food to eat during pregnancy. I think 10 each was too few really. If I'd done more it might have equalled out more.

I wrote the answers on a chart. I felt quite important doing it. It took me just over 2 hours. I also found out that 2 out of 20 women have premature babies. (Babies under 5½ pounds). I didn't know it was so common.

Self Assessment

I had to change one weight from Kg to pounds and ounces. I did it by doing a sum like this.

$$\begin{array}{r} 2 \cdot 4 \\ \times 4 \\ \hline 7 \cdot 0 \end{array}$$

It wasn't difficult to do. I really enjoyed it. My handwriting is untidy. I should have copied it out. I hope I get good marks.

Some investigations by professional researchers

1 How do children learn?

Jean Piaget was a Swiss psychologist born in 1896. He died in the 1970s having contributed much to our understanding about how children think and learn. Many books have been written about him, his ideas and his research. He developed his theories about how children learn by observing them and running simple experiments to see how children would react to certain problems he set them. His complex theory suggests that children's minds develop in stages and that every child must go through each stage to reach the next. He describes how most children reach the next stage at approximately the same age, but of course, there are always individual children who progress through them quicker or slower than others. He believed that children actively try to make sense of their world. The four stages he described are:

(a) **Sensori-motor period** (birth – 2 years)
Children make sense of their world by building up a picture from using their senses and movements. They begin to make simple associations in their minds; eg, smell of milk = time to suck.

(b) **Pre-operational period**
(i) 2–4 years
Children regard everything only in relation to themselves. They are unable to take the viewpoint of other people. They have started to classify objects but only by one important feature. For example, if children of this age watch a demonstration of things that float or sink and the objects were a red brick, a white paper boat, a piece of balsa wood and a carrot, they might predict, if asked, that a red flower will sink and a white marble will float. They think it is the colour of objects that determines buoyancy.

(ii) 4–7 years
Children are now able to classify objects, but the system they use to do it is intuitive. For example, if you ask children of this age to sort out a box of buttons, the result might be a mixture of different classificatory systems. They might sort some according to their colour, others by size or texture. If you talked to the children about their classification system they would probably be unable to explain it to you. Children at this stage are beginning to see relationships between objects and handle simple ideas about numbers, but these are also at an intuitive level so the children cannot explain the process.

(c) **Period of concrete operations** (7–11 years)
Children can now classify and order objects and explain their logic; eg, 'I put this before that one because it is smaller.'

(d) **Period of formal operations** (11–15 years)
Children are now increasingly able to think in an abstract way. They can move ideas around in their minds without needing the objects with them to do it. So a child of this age is able to answer a question such as 'If A is bigger than B and C is bigger than A, which is the biggest?' At this stage, children should be

able to hypothesise; eg, 'What would happen if I . . . ?'

Piaget devised a series of tasks to investigate the intellectual development of children at the stage of concrete operations. He wanted to find out whether children could recognise that certain measurements of objects and substances are not changed by altering their appearance. He called this intellectual ability *Conservation*. Look carefully at the following chart to understand what he found out.

Type of Conservation	Child mentally sees	Experimenter then transforms display	Child is asked conservation question
Length	Two sticks of equal length and agrees that they are of equal length.	Moves stick over.	*Which stick is longer?* *Preconserving* child will say that one of the sticks is longer. *Conserving* child will say that they are both the same length.
Liquid quantity	Two beakers filled with water and says that they both contain the same amount of water.	Pours water from *B* into a tall, thin beaker *C*, so that water level in *C* is higher than in *A*.	*Which beaker has more water?* *Preconserving* child will say that *C* has more water: "See, it's higher" *Conserving* child will say that they have the same amount of water: "You only poured it!"
Substance amount	Two identical clay balls and acknowledges that the two have equal amounts of clay.	Rolls out one of the balls.	*Do the two pieces have the same amount of clay?* *Preconserving* child will say that the long piece has more clay. *Conserving* child will say that the two pieces have the same amount of clay.
Area	Two identical sheets of cardboard with wooden blocks placed on them in identical positions. The child acknowledges that the same amount of space is left open on each piece of cardboard.	Scatters the blocks on one piece of cardboard.	*Do the two pieces of cardboard have the same amount of open space?* *Preconserving* child will say that the cardboard with scattered blocks has less open space. *Conserving* child will say that both pieces have the same amount of open space.

- The people who don't agree with Piaget's theories believe that children can do some of these things but their language development hinders the demonstration of their abilities. Others believe that some of the responses the children made were to please the experimenter, that children always try to work out what adults want them to say.

You could try some of these experiments with children and see whether you get the same responses as Piaget did.
- Can you see any connection between Piaget's stages of intellectual development and the structure of the British education system?

2 Does love and attention help children to progress?

An American psychologist and his associates discovered an interesting idea by accident. Two very young babies who appeared to be mentally retarded when they were in a state orphanage improved dramatically when they transferred to a residential institution for mentally retarded women. On investigating how this had happened, he found that the young children had been given more affection and attention by the mentally retarded women than had been possible from the staff in the overcrowded orphanage. This all happened in the 1930s when the effect of the environment on child development was not really understood.

He decided to experiment further. He persuaded the authorities concerned to allow a further thirteen children between the ages of seven and thirty months old to move from a state orphanage into the institution for the mentally deficient. All these children in the experimental group were apparently mentally retarded, they were very backward in developing the 'normal' milestones achieved by most children. The seven-month-old could scarcely hold his head up and the thirty-month-old child could not stand unaided.

Another group of twelve children in the state orphanage were used as his control group. These children were of roughly the same ages, came from the same sorts of homes and their backgrounds showed no major differences to those of the experimental group.

He found, as in his accidental discovery earlier, that the children in the experimental group flourished, gaining abilities they seemed to be lacking before, whereas the control group seemed to lose even more ground as they grew older. He decided that the difference was the result of much love and attention lavished on those children by the older women in the institution. It soon became clear that each child had acquired a particular adult who was especially attached to them. The children left in the orphanage had a quite different environment with hardly any encouragement or stimulation from the workers there.

In 1966, with considerable difficulty in locating them, the psychologist investigated both groups as adults to see whether the early improvements in the experimental group had persisted into adult life.

He discovered that the experimental group had fared much better than the control group. He found clear differences in the educational attainment, occupational status and general lifestyle. The children from the experimental group had been adopted in childhood, had achieved school-leaving qualifications, got good jobs and most were living in a married and settled lifestyle. The children from the control group, with one exception, were either unemployed and still residents of a state institution or employed in low-paid, unskilled work having achieved very little from the education system. Only a few of this group were in a stable relationship. The one exception in the control group had achieved well at school. A hearing loss had been diagnosed and he was given special education in a school for the deaf. The matron of this residential school had given him special care and attention because he had no family. He was, in the 1960s, in good employment and married with four children. He owned his own home in a comfortable, middle-class district and was earning as much money as all the other people in the control group put together.

The researcher concluded that if children are provided with the chance to develop close, permanent relationships then a bad early experience can be overcome.

- What are the conditions like nowadays for children who live in residential care? Can you find out if they get the chance to make close and permanent relationships with their adult carers?
- What does this research say about all the information one reads concerning early mother–child bonding?
- What do you think happens to a child who has made very close bonds with the adults of the family only to be suddenly deprived of their company? Does the security they have known continue to help them adapt to new circumstances?

3 What causes anti-social behaviour in children?

Michael Rutter, an English psychiatrist, studied the difficulties faced by families when one parent became mentally ill. He was particularly interested to discover whether the separation caused by hospital treatment of the sick family member from the child or children led to anti-social behaviour in the children. This was at a time, in the early 1970s, when it was a commonly held view that a 'broken home' led to delinquent behaviour by the children of that situation.

His study was an epidemiological one; that is, a study where he used existing data collected for a different purpose. He used this data to compare the distribution of disorders in the community with how the distribution varies with particular environmental circumstances. An example of this would be the study of childhood leukaemia and the suggestion that this is more common in parts of the country where nuclear reactors are sited.

Rutter used data from a survey of families on the Isle of Wight and from a representative group of London families. Each family had children between 9–12 years and had one or both parents under psychiatric care. He found that having a parent away from home due to mental illness was a potential cause of short-term distress but that separation did not cause long-term disorder. What seemed to cause problems was the family discord which precedes and accompanies the separation.

He concluded that active discord and lack of affection are associated with anti-social behaviour in the children, but that a good relationship with one parent oftens lessens the effect of a quarrelsome and unhappy home.

- Does this mean that anti-social behaviour by children is the parents' fault?
- What do you think about a proposal to punish parents for the bad behaviour of their children?
- What other influences on children might result in anti-social behaviour?

4 Do parents need to learn from teachers how they should be helping their children?

Barbara Tizard and Martin Hughes wrote *Young Children Learning* (Fontana, 1984) to describe a study they had made about the ways that children learn from their mothers at home. The study questions the widely held view that educationalists have much to teach parents on how to educate and bring up their children. The researchers had a hunch that teachers could also learn from parents.

They were interested in four things: what children were learning at home; whether differences in learning at home were associated with social class differences; what skills and abilities were demonstrated by the children at home; and what were the main differences between the teaching that mothers and nursery teachers provided.

They used only 30 children, all girls. Fifteen of the children came from middle-class homes and fifteen from working-class homes. They selected children who were within three months of their fourth birthday and were attending a morning nursery class or school and spent the afternoons with their mothers at home. The children had all spent at least one term in the nursery class. The eventual selection was composed of children from nine different nursery schools. In order to be able to make fair comparisons between the two groups of children, they excluded families where English was a second language and families consisting of more than three children.

They used audiorecording techniques to record all the verbal interaction used by the child/mother and child/teacher, and an observer to note how the verbal record linked to the activity that was happening at the time. For each child, recordings were made of three 2½-hour sessions at school and two 2½-hour sessions at home. The first morning's recording was discarded, it being a practice for the child, the adult and the observer.

To prevent the mothers and the teachers being self-conscious, they were told that the study was about language development in four-year-olds. The recordings and observations were then analysed carefully by the researchers.

This is what they found out:

(a) The children were learning a lot at home about a vast range of topics and especially about the social world. Because the children at home could have the undivided attention of the mother, even young children were being taught skills that would be difficult for a teacher to teach a large group of children. The learning at home was not artificially provided and this contrasted with school learning.

(b) Working-class mothers were just as keen as middle-class mothers to teach their children. There was some evidence of differences in values, attitudes and priorities between the groups. These differences were one of language style and educational approach rather than any deficit in working-class homes.

(c) Children's questions were the trigger for the mothers' responses which developed into the kind of dialogue that helped children learn, whereas in schools it was the teacher asking all the questions.

(d) Teacher/child conversations at school were more likely to be about the present; those at home meandered into the past and the future. The teacher/child conversations set in the present were less likely to introduce the child to new ideas that develop their minds.

(e) The working-class four-year-olds behaved differently at school than they did at home. At school they became more subdued, passive and less independent. The teachers responded to this by believing them to be less mature than their middle-class peers and this led to the teachers choosing to lower the level of the language they used with them. They had lower expectations of their being able to understand.

They concluded that parents do not need to be taught by the teachers and that teachers could learn a lot from the parents. Tizard and Hughes do not believe that nursery schools or classes are a bad thing, rather that they provide different opportunities for children to learn how to get on with each other and to transfer skills they have learned at home to different situations. They do believe that their study shows that people who claim that nursery school provision is a way of providing valuable linguistic and intellectual stimulation for pre-school children are mistaken.

- Have you ever been asked a question in a way that made you feel the person was putting you down? How does it make you feel? Can this study throw some light on to what puts some children off school, do you think?
- These researchers used no boys in their study. Do you think mothers talk to sons in the same way as they do to their daughters?

Investigations by students

1 Does a week away from home help 7-year-olds develop independence skills?

A Girl Guide, aged 15 years, had promised to go with the local Brownie pack on a week's holiday during the summer. She decided to use this opportunity to investigate how 7-year-olds, away from their parents for the first time, developed independent living skills over the week. She decided to rate each child's performance on a series of behaviours. She did this at the end of each day, attempting to measure any improvement. She rated them on their ability to wash and dress themselves efficiently, whether they cleaned their teeth without a reminder, their ability to make their own beds and look after their own possessions. She also rated them on their helpfulness to

others and their general need for support during the day.

She found that a few of the seven-year-olds made little progress because they were already able to look after themselves quite well. Most of the children did, however, make progress over the week, though not always on each measure.

She was able to use a simple graph to express her results, as the rating scale she had used was a numerical one. She awarded a 5 for totally achieving the criterion and 0 for total inability to do the skill. In her evaluation she recognised that she had used only a small number of children as a sample and that one could not make general conclusions from her study. She also decided that the measure on general need for support could have been influenced by whether or not the children knew her prior to the holiday. She knew three of the children quite well. She did wonder whether the children managed to continue with these skills once they returned back home to the usual family routines.

2 What are the problems for babysitters?

A seventeen-year-old student studying for a BTEC qualification in Caring decided to investigate the best way to go about working as a babysitter. She used her own experience of babysitting to design a questionnaire that surveyed the babysitting experiences of 25 young people. She compared the problems, the pleasures and the financial gains of different babysitting situations. She found that the worst problems were due to difficulties in controlling children they did not know very well, knowing how and when to contact the parents and the lack of medical and first-aid knowledge which caused anxious moments to the young adults involved. The pleasures most often expressed in the responses to the questionnaire were rarely due to the presence of children, but were rather more to do with the benefits of having a quiet place of work, talk, use of the telephone and being able to choose which TV programmes to watch. She evaluated the study by producing a babysitter's manual intended to help parents and prospective babysitters. Comments by users of the manual were included in the appendix to her report.

3 What did and do children wear?

A girl of 14 did an investigation as part of a module on child-related studies. She chose to compare children's clothing at the end of the last century with those available in the late 1980s. She did this by visiting two museums in London: the Victoria and Albert Museum and the Museum of Childhood. She also visited a Mothercare shop. She researched early and present-day photographs.

She found that children were more likely to wear easy care clothing nowadays. She also found that children at the turn of the last century were likely to be easily distinguished as coming from a wealthy or a poor family by looking at the clothes they wore. Children from wealthy families wore more garments at the same time than did the children of poor families who were often scantily dressed even in very cold weather. Clothes were more likely to be mended, home-made and altered a hundred years ago. Today's clothes for children were often mass-produced and commonly bought from chain stores. She felt she did not know enough to compare the comparative costs of the clothing.

4 How do you communicate with deaf people?

A boy of 17, studying on a CPVE course, investigated communicating with deaf people. He had been given a holiday job working in a community centre that catered for a large number of deaf people who lived in a residential centre nearby. Knowing that he would have to be able to communicate with them when they joined in the many activities the community centre provided, the student decided to find out how to do it effectively. He read several books about being deaf and interviewed the social worker responsible for the welfare of the deaf residents. He also made a visit to a school for deaf children and observed them learning to lip-read with their teachers.

He found that whilst younger deaf people had probably learned to lip-read, older deaf people were more likely to use sign language. He found out how to help those who can lip-read by always facing them when communicating with them. He also discovered that his own speech was difficult to lip-read because he tended to mumble.

He came to the conclusion that if he was to be any real use in his holiday job he must speak more clearly and, if possible, learn at least a little sign language.

As a result of the investigation he enrolled at an evening course and learned some sign language. His evaluation was a short video-recording of him 'talking' with a group of delighted deaf people.

5 How will young children react when visiting an adult hospital ward?

A 15-year-old was in hospital at the time her teacher had set as a deadline for a coursework investigation for GCSE. She decided to use the circumstances she found herself in to develop an investigational idea. She had a hunch that her two small sisters, aged 3 and 5 years, would get very excited if they were allowed to visit her. She felt sure that the strange surroundings would make them nervous and she knew how they normally behaved when they were nervous. She decided to observe their reactions to the hospital ward and herself on the one visit they made. Knowing that she could not both record her observations and interact with them she planned to do a retrospective recording of what she had observed. She found that she had been entirely wrong about how her young sisters would behave. For the first time she observed her sisters sitting very quietly and saying hardly anything. She noticed that they wouldn't come near her in the bed and they clung to her mother when she suggested they kiss their big sister. She also noticed how they ignored her when it was time to go, almost dragging their mother along in their haste to get out of the ward.

This pupil concluded that either she had not been right in the past when she judged a certain type of reaction was an indication of her sisters' nervousness in new situations or that they had different reactions for different levels of nervousness.

Nothing she had observed made her understand whether it was the surroundings or herself in a strange orthopaedic contraption that worried them. She therefore asked her mother to try a little experiment. With the ward sister's agreement the mother took the young sisters to see an uncle in another ward in the same hospital. The mother noted that the children behaved outrageously, eating all the grapes, bouncing up and down on the bed and chattering non-stop. The uncle was not tied up with pulleys and weights and counterbalances.

The pupil decided that this further visit to the hospital proved it was the sight of their elder sister in all that strange equipment that had frightened them.

In her evaluation, she explained how her investigation had been limited by her circumstances but thought it was interesting enough to plan a further one when she was discharged from hospital. She thought her further study could ask parents whether they knew if their children were particularly anxious and what made them think so.

6 Why are parents still buying commercial baby foods when they are being tampered with?

A 14-year-old pupil was shocked by the news of babies being injured as a result of criminal tampering with commercial baby foods. He learned from the TV coverage of the news story that some shops were not withdrawing the tins and jars from their shelves and that parents were apparently still buying them. He decided to investigate if this was true and if so, why parents were prepared to take the risk. With the permission of the supermarket manager who had approved his questionnaire, he surveyed eighteen women and two men who took the suspect goods off the shelves and put them in their trolleys. He found out from the manager that had there not been the present scare many more people would have been choosing to buy the products.

He discovered that most of the purchasers were, indeed, worried by the possibility of contamination. Only one of the customers thought the scare had been 'blown up out of all proportion'. When he asked the other nineteen why they still bought the commercial baby foods, 75 per cent of them revealed that they did not know what else they could feed their baby with. The other 25 per cent said that their babies were such fussy eaters that they had refused the homemade food they had prepared as an alternative and that they were buying the products in desperation because their babies were miserable without them.

In his conclusion this pupil stated that whilst most parents had been put off buying the suspect goods, the few who were taking a risk did so mostly out of ignorance. He felt that the manufacturers concerned should have produced a helpful leaflet, and that demonstrations could have been arranged to show parents how to prepare suitable alternatives. He also concluded that every pupil in school should be taught how to prepare meals for all age groups as part of their education.

In his evaluation he wished he had included a question in his survey to find out whether the twenty people had, in fact, learned about food preparation at school. Perhaps they had, but had forgotten.

7 Do human sensory abilities change as one gets older?

A 15-year-old pupil doing a GCSE investigation learned on her course that very young children learned through their senses. She wondered whether human sensory abilities change over a lifetime. She decided to investigate this. Using her 5-year-old brother, her 19-year-old brother, her mother and her grandmother, she devised a set of tests to give them. She tested their hearing, sight, sense of touch, smell and taste.

The hearing test was to sit the subject (person who is being tested) in the middle of the room, blindfolded and facing the window. She asked the subject to listen carefully and when she clapped her hands to point in the direction the noise came from. She did this from different points in the room ten times. She gave each of her subjects a point for each successful indication of where the noise was made.

The sight test was simple. She had ten small objects in a bag so that the subject could not see them. Again she asked the subject to sit down, this time in the garden which was long and thin. She started two steps away from the subject, took an object from her bag and placed it in the palm of her hand in front of her. She asked the subject to name or describe each object. She moved two steps further away each time. She recorded one point for each object correctly identified.

The touch test was a blindfolded recognition by touch of everyday objects with different textures. Again there were ten objects and the subject scored one point for each correct identification.

For the test of smell, she prepared ten small jars covered in an opaque sticky paper. She punctured the lids so that the smell of the ten different substances they contained could filter through the holes. To be absolutely sure that her subjects would not get any visual clues to help them she used a blindfold. Correctly identified smells scored one point.

For the final test of taste, she prepared ten foods and puréed them so that they had a similar texture. She then blindfolded the subjects and gave them a taste of each food to identify. A correct identification scored one point.

Her investigation took a long time to prepare and carry out. It was important that the subjects were tested individually. She asked them to keep the tests a secret so that her results were as fair as possible. For this reason she tested her 5-year-old brother last on each test, knowing that he found it virtually impossible to keep a secret.

Her results were presented in graphical form as she had used a numerical scoring system.

She found that the youngest and the oldest people had the most difficulties with the tests. She suggested that they might be for different reasons. She thought that her grandmother's sensory abilities were failing due to old age, but that her young brother had not achieved as well as her elder brother and her mother because he might not have understood what to do properly. She also thought that his lack of experience with different tastes and smells might have caused the result. She wondered whether his language ability affected his ability to name or describe objects.

Her evaluation recognised how small her sample was and how complicated it had been trying to make the tests fair. She also pointed out that an incidental result had been the discovery of her elder brother's inability to visually discriminate between objects at a distance. Her brother had not realised this before and he now wears glasses prescribed by the optician he saw as a result of his sister's GCSE work.

Exercises in converting data into graphical form

1 Favourite books

100 children were asked to name their favourite story book.

Half of the children asked were boys. All the children were within three months of their fifth birthday.

The results

25 girls	3 boys	chose	*My Little Sister*
6 girls	20 boys	chose	*Thomas the Tank Engine*
12 girls	17 boys	chose	*Charlie and the Chocolate Factory*
6 girls	4 boys	chose	*Mrs Pepperpot*
1 girl	4 boys	chose	*Peter Rabbit*
0 girls	2 boys	did not have a favourite story book.

(a) Draw a pie-chart to show the overall popularity of these books.
(b) Draw two separate pie-charts to show the difference between the choices that the girls and boys made.
(c) What reasons might there be for a child of this age not to have a favourite story?
(d) Can you depict this information in an alternative graphical form?

2 Travelling to school

Parents were asked to record the time in minutes that it took them to travel from their front door to the nursery school their child attended. The purpose of the study was to find out if a collection service would be useful for the parents. As the parents arrived they just wrote down in a numbered slot how long it had taken.

The results

Child	Time	Child	Time
1	15	16	11
2	13½	17	12
3	10	18	4
4	5	19	3
5	6	20	4½
6	6½	21	12
7	17	22	15
8	25	23	16½
9	4	24	5½
10	6	25	15
11	12	26	14½
12	11½	27	7½
13	10	28	7
14	9	29	16
15	9½	30	11

(a) Describe the *range* of times taken by these parents.
(b) What is the *mode* of these times?
(c) What is the *median* of these times?
(d) What is the *average* time?
(e) Is there a way of depicting this information as a graph? You could categorize each journey as short; middling; long.
(f) Do these figures mean that Child no. 19 lives nearest to the school and no. 8 lives furthest away? Give reasons for your answer.

(g) Was this a useful study? Is there a better way of deciding whether a collection service would be useful?

3 Newborn babies

Percentage of under-fives attending pre-school provision

22%
Nursery School or Class

21%
Primary Infant Class

42%
Playgroup

Some graphical information can be made most attractive by using a pictogram as above. The same information is used as in a histogram, but it looks more decorative.

Draw a pictogram that shows the gender difference in the average length of newborn babies.

| No. | Birth length in inches | |
---	Boys	Girls
1	21	22
2	23	20
3	22½	20½
4	24	20
5	20	21
6	22	22½
7	23	21½
8	22½	21
9	21	23
10	24½	19

4 Sentencing children

(a) Draw a graph to show the decline in the number of juveniles found guilty by all courts in England and Wales between 1981 and 1986.

The age of criminal responsibility is 10 years (England and Wales) and 8 years (Scotland). There are differences in the legal and judicial systems of England/Wales, Scotland and Northern Ireland.
The term juvenile is not used after attaining the age of 17 (England and Wales) or 16 (Scotland). The age group 17–20 are known as young adults in England and Wales.

England and Wales

Sentencing

Juveniles found guilty by all courts (indictable offences) *(thousands)*

		1981	1985	1986
Males	10–13	15.1	9.1	6.1
	14–16	62.3	48.1	37.7
Females	10–13	1.8	0.9	0.5
	14–16	7.5	5.0	3.7

(b) Why are there no figures for children under the age of ten?
(c) Which group of children are more likely to be found guilty in the courts?

5 English as a second language

In 1987 the Inner London Education Authority published the information below about the languages spoken by some of the many pupils in their schools.

On a survey done by their Research and Statistics branch they found that 172 individual languages were being spoken by

64,987 speakers. For these children English was their second language. The main language groups were:

%	Language	%	Language
26.1	Bengali	4.0	Greek
6.9	Turkish	3.6	French
6.7	Chinese	3.1	Yomba
6.0	Gujerati	3.0	Portugese
5.9	Urdu	2.9	Italian
5.0	Spanish	1.6	Vietnamese
4.9	Punjabi	15.5	All other
4.7	Arabic		language groups

(Figures taken from ILEA: Education Statistics, 1988–1989)

(a) Put this information into a suitable graphic form.
(b) Can you think of another way of expressing the same information? Could you do a world map with the continents acting as a base for the percentages?
(c) Can you speak more than one language? Can you speak another language well enough to be taught all your lessons in that other language? There is a school in London that teaches all its pupils in all subjects using French. Why might that be a good idea for your school?

6 Child abuse

Read the following article about the NSPCC's annual report 1988.

NSPCC report

Sex abuse cases up by 24%

By Ruth Gledhill

Child sexual abuse referrals to the NSPCC increased by 24 per cent last year but referrals of other abuse decreased.

The children's charity appealed for more donations after ending the year with a £3 million-plus deficit and record levels of spending.

"We have got to get ourselves into the position where our income meets expenditure", Dr Alan Gilmour, the NSPCC director, said.

The figures showed that fears that the Cleveland sex abuse affair would sweep what had always been a difficult area back under the carpet were unfounded, he said.

"We are obviously going to have to do something about the area of neglect because the referral rate has been slipping down. Neglect has again become a neglected area.

"Sexual abuse is not the only area of child misery."

The charity reported that its target of setting up 60 child protection teams in five years had been reached on schedule.

It spent £18.28 million on services to children, a 25 per cent increase on the year before last.

There were 2,876 referrals of sexual abuse, 4,519 of physical abuse, 1,684 of emotional abuse, 3,365 of children being left alone, and 4,907 of neglect. The last two were down by about 1,000 each on the year before.

In more than 95 per cent of the cases the NSPCC found good reasons for the referral, although the abuse was not always of the type stated.

Out of more than 21,000 referrals involving 42,853 children, more than half were from the public, 18 per cent from parents and 16 per cent from officials. Only 255 were from the children themselves.

(a) Draw a graph to show the numerical differences in the types of abuse that were referred to them.
(b) Draw a graph showing where the referrals came from.
(c) As there were 21,000 referrals involving 42,853 children, some referrals must have been about more than one child. Why would this happen? What must be the average number of children involved with each referral?

7 Brownie points

This is the data recorded by the pupil who did the investigation described on page 115.

Brownie (identified by initial)	Wash + dress	Teeth	Bed – making	Possessions	Helpfulness	Need for support	Progress Day 6 – Day 1
A	15	18	20	10	28	20	+9
C	20	18	19	15	26	18	+5
L	30	30	30	30	28	30	0
F	19	18	20	20	18	18	+6
G	15	18	20	19	14	23	+10
H	20	19	22	19	24	25	+3
S	15	14	20	12	26	20	+20
M	28	29	30	28	30	30	0
MD	20	20	19	18	28	18	+8
J	18	16	19	12	30	24	+12
JP	14	10	11	8	18	12	-4
D	12	13	18	19	20	10	+14

(a) Which Brownies were the ones already very skilled and independent for their age?

(b) Draw a graph to show the overall differences in the Brownies' independent behaviour.

(c) Draw a graph showing the progress made by the Brownies.

(d) Which Brownie was worse rather than better at the end of the week? Can you suggest reasons for this?

(e) Which skill were the Brownies best at overall?

(f) Can you think of a fairer way to measure their progress?

8 Human sensory abilities

This is the data of the 15-year-old GCSE pupil who investigated sensory abilities over four different age groups. You can read the investigation on pages 118–19.

Subjects	Sight	Hearing	Tests Touch	Smell	Taste	Total
Little brother	4	5	4	6	4	23
Big brother	3	9	10	10	9	41
Mother	8	8	9	10	10	45
Grandmother	5	4	8	7	6	30

(a) Draw a graph to show the sensory abilities of this family.

(b) Which test was performed best overall?

(c) Which test was performed least well overall?

(d) What was the average difference between the male and female scores? Can you express that as a graph?

9 Child sex abuse: the Cleveland cases

Read the following newspaper article:

Doctor's concern as five Cleveland cases are reopened

By Peter Davenport

A consultant paediatrician at the centre of the Cleveland child sexual abuse crisis said yesterday that he was concerned at disclosures that some of the children who were returned to their parents were again under investigation.

Dr Geoffrey Wyatt who, with Dr Marietta Higgs, made the diagnoses that led to the crisis, was speaking after Cleveland County Council confirmed that five of the 123 children whose cases were considered by the public inquiry under Lord Justice Butler-Sloss had since been referred to the social services on suspicion of having been sexually abused again.

Dr Wyatt, who was reprimanded by his employers, the Northern Regional Health Authority, and forbidden from working on cases of child sexual abuse, said yesterday: "My concerns have always been, and will always be, the children of Cleveland. If these figures of re-referrals are correct then, of course, it does concern me."

The confirmation of the figures was also seized upon by supporters of the two consultants to support their campaign to have Dr Higgs, who was seconded to work in a Newcastle maternity hospital at the end of the public inquiry, re-instated.

Dr Peter Morrell, a consultant paediatrician who is based at the Middlesbrough General Hospital, was among 11 north-east doctors who expressed their support publicly for the doctors earlier this year. He said: "This is further confirmation of our belief that the cases were correctly diagnosed originally and of our fears that children who were sent home may have been sent back to further abuse."

Dr Higgs is appealing against a High Court refusal to grant her an injunction against the Northern Regional Health Authority, preventing it from imposing disciplinary action against her.

The disclosure was something that senior council officials had been concerned about in the aftermath of the public inquiry.

They believed that a "roller coaster" of public opinion had helped to sway decisions by courts and that some children who had been abused were being returned home without any legal protection and could face further abuse.

Yesterday Cleveland County Council said that the figures emerged as it was gathering data requested by the Government.

A spokesman said: "All the re-referrals were for suspicion of alleged sexual abuse."

According to reports yesterday, the statistics showed that of the 123 children originally involved, 36 were still wards of court, although 25 of those were at home under supervision orders. Five were in foster care, one in residential placement and one under voluntary supervision. In four of the wardship cases there was no further social services involvement.

Of the children who were not made wards of court, 24 were at home under continuing care or supervision orders, nine others were in foster care, four were in residential placements and a further two with foster parents.

At the time the information was prepared for ministers, 48 of the children were said to be no longer in contact with social services. Twenty of them had been sent home under supervision, which had since ended, and the remaining 28 had been returned to their homes by courts with no supervision orders and the families apparently cleared.

The five children who have been re-referred are all thought to have come from that last group.

The re-referrals are understood to have come from agencies outside the social services department and although social workers are investigating the cases, none of the children have been removed from their homes.

The Northern Regional Health Authority said yesterday that it could not comment on the new disclosures because of the impending legal action with Dr Higgs.

(a) Draw a pie-chart showing the number of children now back home, those in foster care, and those in residential care.

(b) Draw a histogram showing how many of these children are still receiving some social services support.

(c) What should children do if they are being abused? Who should they go to for help?

(d) What would you do if you had strong reasons to believe a child was being abused at home?

10 Reading development

Stages of reading development: an outline of the major qualitative characteristics and how they are acquired

1 Stage designation	2 Grade range (age)	3 Major qualitative characteristics and masteries by end of age	4 How acquired	5 Relationship of reading to listening
Stage 0: Prereading, 'pseudo-reading'	Preschool ages 6 months–6 years	Child 'pretends' to read, retells story when looking at pages of book previously read to him/her; names letters of alphabet; recognizes some signs; prints own name; plays with books, pencils and paper.	Being read to by an adult (or older child) who responds to and warmly appreciates the child's interest in books and reading; being provided with books, paper, pencils, blocks and letters.	Most can understand the children's picture books and stories read to them. They understand thousands of words they hear by age 6 but can read few if any of them.
Stage 1: Initial reading and decoding	Grade 1 & beginning Grade 2 (ages 6 & 7)	Child learns relation between letters and sounds and between printed and spoken words; child is able to read simple text containing high frequency words and phonically regular words; uses skill and insight to 'sound out' new one-syllable words.	Direct instruction in letter-sound relations (phonics) and practice in their use. Reading of simple stories using words with phonic elements taught and words of high frequency. Being read to on a level above what child can read independently to develop more advanced language patterns, knowledge of new words and ideas.	The level of difficulty of language read by the child is much below the language understood when heard. At the end of stage 1, most children can understand up to 4000 or more words when heard but can read only about 600.
Stage 2: Confirmation and fluency	Grades 2 & 3 (ages 7 & 8)	Child reads simple, familiar stories and selections with increasing fluency. This is done by consolidating the basic decoding elements, sight vocabulary and meaning context in the reading of familiar stories and selections.	Direct instruction in advanced decoding skills; wide reading (with instruction and independently) of familiar, interesting materials which help promote fluent reading. Being read to at levels above their own independent reading level to develop language, vocabulary and concepts.	At the end of stage 2, about 3000 words can be read and understood and about 9000 are known when heard. Listening is still more effective than reading.

(a) Draw a graph showing the relationship between reading and listening in children 6–8 years.

(b) Describe how parents could help their child to learn to read.

(c) Explain why children should learn lower case letters before upper case ones.

Further reading

There are many books available about the development and care of children. Your local library should be a good source for getting started on some extra reading about childhood.

If you particularly want to read more about some of the ideas in the assignments in this book the following chart might get you started.

Content	Assignment	Resources/books
Child abuse	Investigation 8, pp. 23–27	*Water Babies*, by Erik Sidenbladh (Fontana, 1982). This book describes the work of Igor Tjarkovsky.
		NSPCC Annual Report. Free from 67 Saffron Hill, London EC1N 8RS. A4 s.a.e. appreciated, as is donation to funds.
		NCH Annual Review. Free from NCH, 85 Highbury Park, London N5 1UD. A4 s.a.e. appreciated, as is donation to funds.
		The Case against Smacking, by Penelope Leach and Peter Newell of EPOCH (End Physical Punishment of Children). Free from EPOCH, PO Box 962, London N22 UX. A4 s.a.e. appreciated.
Rights of children	Investigations 1, pp. 8–10, and 8, pp. 23–27	*Convention on the Rights of the Child* and education pack available from UNICEF, Education Department, 55 Lincoln's Inn Fields, London WC2A 3NB.
Children and advertising	Investigation 13, pp. 38–39	The British Code of Advertising Practice. Project kit for 8–14-year-olds explains how inappropriate advertising is stopped by the Committee of Advertising Practice. Available from CAP, Brook House, 2–16 Torrington Place, London WC1E 7HN. £1.00 to cover postage and costs.
History of childhood	Investigation 12, pp. 34–37	*A Child's World: A Social History of English Childhood, 1800–1914*, by James Walvin (Penguin Books, 1982)
	Investigation 8, pp. 23–27	*Centuries of Childhood*, by Philippe Aries (Penguin, 1962). Chapter 4 on Play is particularly useful.

Content	Assignment	Resources/books
Wolf children	Investigation 3, pp. 11–13	*The Wolf Children*, by Charles Maclean (Allen Lane, 1977) *The Forbidden Experiment: The Story of the Wild Boy of Aveyron*, by Roger Shattuck (Secker and Warburg, 1980)
The effects of deprivation in the early years of childhood	Investigation 3, pp. 11–13 Some investigations done by professional researchers, pp. 110–14	*Early Experience: Myth and Evidence*, by Ann M. Clarke and A. D. B. Clarke (Open Books Publishing, 1976)
Piaget	Some investigations done by professional researchers, pp. 110–14 Investigation 5 pp. 16–19	Both these books have particularly useful chapters on his work: *Children: Development through Adolescence*, by Alison Clarke-Stewart and Joanne Barbara Koch (Wiley, 1983) esp. Chapter 10. *Child Development: A First Course*, by Kathy Sylva and Ingrid Lunt (Grant McIntyre, 1982) esp. Chapter 7.
Learning to read	Investigation 5 pp. 16–19	*Understanding Child Development*, by Sara Meadows (Hutchinson, 1986) esp. Chapter 3.

Dear Teacher/Lecturer

This book is an attempt to help you plan an active course for the students you teach. I expect you have many content-laden books to use with your planning. I have divided the book into sections to assist you to 'pick and mix' as you plan to deliver your course objectives and syllabus. The three sections are entitled 'Investigations', 'Technological Assignments' and 'Methodology'.

The 'Investigations' section is a series of assignments based on fundamental issues relating to childhood. They are of a philosophical, social, economic, physical, emotional, political and moral nature and should encourage your students to examine them critically. They are designed to be suitable learning experiences that can be incorporated into GCSE courses, Personal, Social and Health Education programmes and TVEI modules on Personal and Social Development. NNEB and BTEC Course Tutors may also find these useful.

The 'Technological Assignments' section includes a series of assignments that should develop an understanding of the technological process and its implications for childhood. A batch of cross-curricular technological assignments are included which could form a basis for an Integrated Technology programme to meet National Curriculum targets.

The final section on Methodology serves to assist students in gaining more rigour in their research activities into the human condition. Whilst the assignments within this section are based in terms of child development, they have been designed to develop basic social science research skills of a more generic nature.

Each assignment is based on the notion that your students come to the classroom with much knowledge about childhood and your role is to act as facilitator, providing a context that allows them to explore that knowledge and add to it; to develop skills that are in their infancy and learn new ones as well; and to explore their own and others' attitudes in order to be able to modify and adjust them.

The role of the teacher as facilitator, rather than as the fount of all knowledge, is a comparatively new one for some teachers. I am only too aware how anxiety-making that can be without practise and the growing confidence it brings. I have, therefore, tried to graduate the amount of teacher and pupil support I have provided within the assignments. I am also aware that many teachers will want to adjust the methodology suggested to suit their own expertise and experience. I have erred on the side of the inexperienced, knowing that those with more confidence will naturally make these ideas their own and deliver them in ways suited to the young people they teach.

Groupwork is an essential ingredient of most of the assignments suggested. I have added some individual ones for those teachers who need them as preparation for examination requirements. It is because the tasks are, in the main, group-targeted that I have been able to provide many stimuli that require a fairly complex level of reading for understanding. It does mean, of course, that groups should be of mixed ability so that the more able readers can assist those less competent to understand the case studies, newspaper cuttings and other textual material. Knowing that some of your students do not enjoy writing for writing's sake, I have tried to provide many tasks that require other skills, hoping that the variety of tasks will motivate them to one of the main aims of the book which is to encourage young people to **think** about the issues appertaining to childhood.

I make no apology for believing in education which I hope will help to fulfil the following assessment aims:

Do the pupils *talk to each other* about their work?

Do they *initiate* activities which are new to the classroom?

Do they *persist* over a period of days, weeks or months on things which capture their interest?

Do they have *real interests* of their own?

Are they able to say 'I don't know' with the expectation that they are going to *do something about finding out*?

Do they exhibit any *initiative*, have they developed any *skill in finding out* what they want to know?

Do they continue to wonder?

Can they *deal with differences of opinion* or differences in beliefs on a reasonably objective basis without being completely swayed by considerations of social status?

Are they capable of *intense involvement*? Have they ever had a *passionate commitment* to anything?

Do they have a *sense of humour* which can find expression in relation to things that are important to them?

Do they continue to *explore* things which are not assigned outside school as well as within?

Can they afford to *make mistakes* freely and profit from them?

Do they *reflect* upon their errors and learn from them?

Do they *challenge ideas and interpretations* with the purpose of reaching deeper understandings?

Are they *charitable and open* in dealing with ideas they do not agree with?

Can they *listen* to each other?

Are they *willing to attempt to express ideas* about which they only have a vague and intuitive awareness?

Are they able to *make connections* between things which seem superficially unrelated?

Are they *flexible* in problem solving?

Are they *willing to argue* with others?

Can they *suspend judgement*?

Are they capable of experiencing *freshly and vividly*?

Do they *know how to get help when they need it* and *refuse help when appropriate*?

Are they *self-propelling*?

Can they *accept guidance* without having to have things prescribed?

Are they *stubborn about holding views which are not popular*?

Can they *deal with distractions*, avoid being at the mercy of the environment?

Are they *intellectually responsible*?

Do they *recognise conflicting evidence* or conflicting points of view?

Do they *recognise their own potential* in growing towards competence?

From *Learning Through Science Aims*, as quoted in *The Practical Curriculum – Primary Phase*,
(Methuen Education for Schools Council, 1981)

I hope, very much, that you will enjoy using this book with your students.

Yours sincerely,

Jennie Petersen

Jennie Petersen